BUILDING WEALTH WITH INNER CITY RENTALS

Success the Catalytic Landlord Way

catalyst

An agent that significantly increases
the rate of a reaction.

catalytic landlord

A rental owner who assumes a leadership
position in a troubled community to quicken
the pace of neighborhood revitalization.

The Catalytic Landlord: Increasing Profits by Accelerating

Neighborhood Revitalization

Published in the United States by Williamson Ideations

Dedication

To Monique, Anaiya and Nayla for their encouragement and
understanding. I love you.

To my Oak Park friends and family who've taught me so much.

And to all my Leading Landlord subscribers that
gave me their input and inspiring words.

Thank you!

CONTENTS

PREFACE:
MY STORY

In 1999 I realized I had created a very small yet vibrant community at my three-unit rental that was located in Sacramento, California. The converted two-story Victorian was located in Midtown Sacramento, a neighborhood that was just completing a revitalization effort; and everyone felt optimistic.

I thought it was interesting that my tenants were taking great care of the place and "didn't want me to worry about things." I was amused they wanted to handle the "chores", do the gardening and help each other. Not until later did I realize their sense of belongingness was off the chart. They were behaving like true stakeholders!

I became bored with my threeplex and increasingly interested in the work St. HOPE Academy was doing in Oak Park, a nearby inner-city community. St. HOPE's mission is to revitalize inner-city communities through public education, civic leadership, economic development and the arts. It was founded by former NBA All Star, Kevin Johnson, who is now the mayor of Sacramento.

In October 1999, I attended a workshop that St. HOPE sponsored where I was introduced to Dr. Michael E. Porter's work. Dr. Porter is a Harvard Business School professor and is widely considered to be the founder of the modern field of business strategy.

Many of the ideas presented in Dr. Porter's Harvard Business Review article, The Competitive Advantage of the Inner-City, resonated with me, but one idea stopped me in my tracks:

"Business people, entrepreneurs, and investors must lead the economic revival; and community activists, social service providers, and government bureaucrats must support them."

What shocked me was that I envisioned myself as a hardwired entrepreneur and I was interested in real estate and leadership as well, but I never saw how it all fit together.

I ended up expanding my definition of a landlord to be more of an entrepreneur than just an investor; a shift which helped me understand that landlords in troubled communities had the potential to be catalysts for economic revival. And once that idea jelled, I took Dr. Porter's words as a personal call to action.

So, in 2002, my wife and I took the plunge and purchased a heavily discounted, crime-ridden, eight-unit apartment building in Oak Park. The building was structurally in good shape but listed for $340,000 even though similar properties in other neighborhoods were priced at $600,000 and up. The complex sat on the market for over a year before I started pursuing it. It was well positioned to benefit from the influence of current and future revitalization projects, but apparently no one wanted to deal with the headache. It was a hub for drug dealing, prostitution – and obviously out of control.

As I worked to stabilize the place, I watched St. HOPE move commercial tenants into a newly redeveloped mixed-use complex called 40 Acres. At the same time, I concluded after attending a few neighborhood association meetings, that very capable community leaders were in place and they were on track to reduce the crime rate.

I was convinced that the community would make a comeback and I wanted to go along for the ride. So in 2005, I left my civil engineering job and began working full time for St. HOPE.

While working as a project manager for St. HOPE Development Company, I had time to read case studies about inner-city redevelopments, attend neighborhood and business association meetings, and embed myself into the community. I introduced myself to as many local leaders as possible and worked hard to connect different groups that had duplicative efforts.

In 2007, St. HOPE sponsored my trip to Harvard Divinity School Summer Leadership Institute where some amazing social entrepreneurs from all over the world gathered and learned about creating action plans. At Harvard I came to understand the power of long-term strategic thinking and how a little upfront planning could help move the obstacles that held communities down.

In 2008 the recession hit, causing ripples that led to me being laid off. Nevertheless, I continued to oversee one of St. HOPE's redevelopment projects: the Guild Theater. I just wasn't willing to stop until the beautifully remodeled theater was up and running.

As a surprise to many, including myself, Oak Park's crime rates didn't skyrocket during the recession. In fact, in the redeveloped areas, the crime rate continued to fall. There was no question about it; Oak Park had turned the corner.

Now, in 2013, several mixed-use buildings are being constructed along our business corridor and our locally owned coffee shop is filled with people who have no idea about the challenges the neighborhood once faced. Soon the neighborhood will be celebrated for triumphing over the stigma placed on it after the 1960 riots.

Also, as a result, I now have over 10,000 hours of experience under my belt – the level of experience many consider as the threshold of expertise. So it is time for me to speak up.

This book summarizes the lessons learned from living through two neighborhood revitalization efforts, along with the education I gained from my involvement with St. HOPE.

It's the guide I wish I could have had from the beginning. It would have saved me time and heartache. May it jumpstart your efforts and help you be a catalyst for the neighborhood you're most passionate about.

CHAPTER 1:
INTRODUCTION

This is a book for double bottom line investors:

– those wanting to make a handsome profit while changing the world for the better.

– It's for folks with thick skin who are willing to be misunderstood until their dream is almost a reality.

– It's also for those who still believe, despite what cynics say, that one person can make a difference. If this sounds like you – great. Let's get started. In the following pages, I will unpack this central idea:

Landlords in troubled neighborhoods can increase their cash flow, property values and quality of tenants by leading a campaign to improve the orderliness of the community surrounding their property.

As a starting point, let's climb up to the balcony and look down on a typical landlord-stakeholder relationship. From high above, the relationships look like this:

As the figure implies, most landlords go about doing business as usual. That is, they try to take care of their property and the tenant who pays the rent. They assume their tenant will be able to build healthy relationships with the surrounding community.

There is certainly nothing wrong with this model. It works fine the majority of the time; and exceptionally well in middle income and wealthier communities.

But, just like with most rules of thumb, there are exceptions; and low income communities that have high crime rates and low owner-occupancy rates are the exception. It's easy to ride a bicycle without hands once it's moving, but nearly impossible to do so when just starting out. So it is with inner-city rentals. It's best not to go hands-free until you have some momentum.

And here's where many inner-city landlords find themselves. They do their research but nearly every book and website teaches them to do business as usual – after there's momentum.

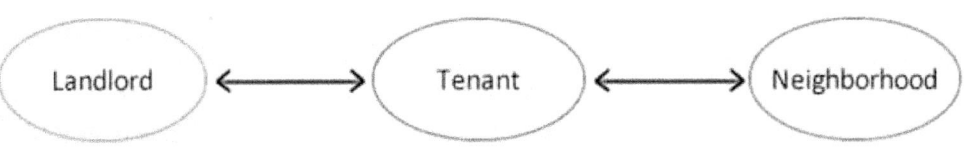

Please don't get me wrong; you can still make a profit doing business as usual with inner-city rentals. However, your property value will be capped by the public's bad perception of the area, and your tenant applicant pool will remain the same. The property will not get any easier to manage, and the cycle of coping and co-existing with unsavory elements will continue. Simply put, you will not gain momentum this way.

Doing business as usual does not improve the status quo. It does not add value to the inner city.

What I'm offering is a way out of that cycle. A landlord can do more than cope with current conditions and utter the first line of the Serenity Prayer:

"God, give me grace to accept with serenity the things that cannot be changed…"

That is not an acceptable business strategy. I'm arguing that this defeatist approach needs to be modified to tap the potential wealth of an underperforming community.

This figure shows the landlord inserting himself into the center of the equation, bridging the relationship with the tenant and the neighborhood.

The landlord works to introduce the neighborhood to the tenant, and vice-versa. This establishes a value economy where the landlord's role becomes less and less important as the neighborhood-tenant relationship strengthens. This way of doing business hinges on the *second* line of the Serenity Prayer:

"God, give me …. the Courage to change the things which should be changed…"

What this book details is shown in the figure below.

LANDLORD-DRIVEN NEIGHBORHOOD REVITALIZATION

Landlord-Driven Neighborhood Revitalization (LDNR) is a strategy that acknowledges that the landlord, tenant and neighborhood are interdependently linked together. Landlords create value by investing time and a tiny amounts of money to strengthen connections and a create self-reinforcing organization that benefit all stakeholders.

So instead of watching a neighborhood spiral downward, a landlord can use a customized LDNR strategy to ensure that it ascends upward.

A landlord using a LDNR strategy MUST NOT be the only entity working towards restoration, but they MUST BE positioned to profit from restoration. They should take an equity position (have a large enough financial stake in the community) so their actions, which may appear as solely charitable, align with objectives that bring about a reduction of the stigma placed on the neighborhood.

In a nutshell, you want to use the LDNR strategy to reduce the discount placed on your troubled rentals so they appraise for nearly the same value as similar properties in "good" markets.

Discounted Values – What You Know but Probably Didn't Know You Knew

Let me clarify this idea of discounted property values by referencing the neighborhoods near you. Somewhere near your home there is a neighborhood that has a premium attached to it; all the fancy people live there and the homes are more expensive associated with a prodigious brand. Even a small dumpy looking house would be priced high just because it was in the right neighborhood.

Well, when it comes to discount properties, I'm talking about the exact opposite. I'm talking about the properties in the not-so good areas near you. Their values are lower because the area's reputation is tarnished. There is a negative premium or discount associated with them. A nice house in this neighborhood would be priced lower than you'd expect just because the area is perceived "unsafe" or "bad."

So if there were identical houses were built in both neighborhoods, the one in the "bad" part of town would be priced below typical market value simply because of the neighborhood's status. That's pretty obvious – right?

Capitalizing On Restoring Discounted Property Values

Well what if there was a way to improve a neighborhood's reputation after you purchased a rental at a discounted price? If you could get your rental to appraise at the typical market value you would make money right? ***Aha! That's how you build wealth with inner city rentals!***

The process is not expensive or complicated once you understand how inner city communities operate. Think of a neighborhood as a group of interconnected people and property owners. From a landlords' perspective a neighborhood can be illustrated as a contraption made from two teeter totters connected by a hinge.

See figure below.

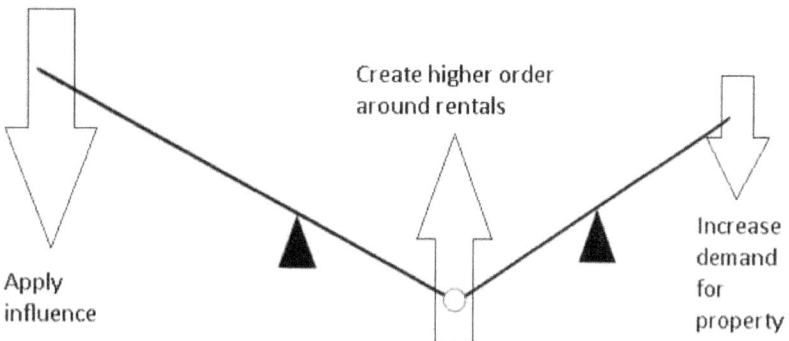

To increase the demand/desirability for your property, you will need to make the area more orderly and ensure basic rules of decency get enforced.

The circle in the middle of the contraption represents the hinge that connects the two teeter totters. Since we want to lower the far right end of the contraption (increase demand), we need to lift the midsection (increase the order around your rentals).

And the good news is that as a landlord in a trouble neighborhood, you have a tremendous amount of influence at your disposal. You can easily apply your influence and make the contraction work in your favor.

A pictorial summary can be found below.

What do you think? Does it seem like a reasonable plan? Do you understand how an investor can buy into a troubled neighborhood and make a lot of money by following this six step process? Well if you're nodding "yes" then you bought the right book!

There is a good amount of theory that I think is really important for you to understand to make a Landlord-Driven Neighborhood Revitalization strategy work for you. However my reviewers told me not to hit you with it up front so I've put that information in the Appendix. But I strongly urge you to read it to deepen your understanding of neighborhood revitalization from a landlord's perspective. Doing so will help you make sound decisions on the fly.

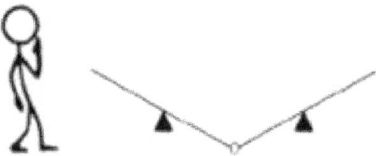

#1 Acquire an inner-city property that's strategically positioned for a successful revitilization campaign.

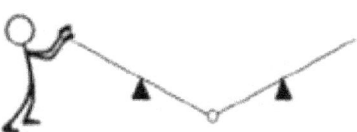

#2 Landlord assumes a leadership role and begins applying influence.

#3 Landlord acts as a catalyst to do things residents are reluctant to do. This gives residents a glimpse of the neighborhood's potential.

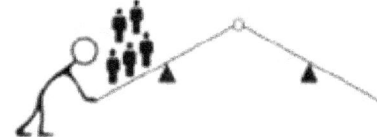

#4 Residents get onboard a bandwagon of success.

#5 Landlord exits after developments justify an increase in demand and outsiders show interest.

#6 Community moves forward as residents and outsiders advance their mutual self-interests.

HERE'S HOW THE BOOK IS LAID OUT

Since the process of rebuilding a neighborhood's brand will take several years, I arrange the book as a travel guide to help you plan for and take an adventure.

Part 1 – The Map

    ○○ **Chapter 2** – Presents a quick introduction of the LDNR Chart.

    ○○ **Chapter 3** – Presents how to use the Chart as a Roadmap.

Part 2 – The Logistics

    ○○ **Chapter 4** – Describes the mechanics behind the neighborhood revitalization investment strategy.

Part 3 – The Journey

    ○○ **Chapter 5** – Suggests tips on where to find properties positioned for successful LDNR campaigns.

    ○○ **Chapter 6** – Discusses how an investor becomes a Catalytic Landlord.

    ○○ **Chapter 7** – Outlines ways to work with others to move forward during the Team Building Stage.

    ○○ **Chapter 8** – Describes ways to promote the area during the Lag Stage.

    ○○ **Chapter 9** – Outlines an approach to exit the investment after the neighborhood has been restored.

Part 4 – Tools For The Trip

    ○○ **Chapter 10** – Discusses a strategy to overcome the resistance you'll face along the journey.

    ○○ **Chapter 11** – Summaries the LDNR key ideas and helps you organize an action plan for your community.

    ○○ **Chapter 12** – Lists additional resources you will need to help you during your journey.

As previously mentioned, in order to put theory into action you'll need to write an action plan to address your community's uniqueness.

Every neighborhood has its own flavor. What was successful in my community may not work in yours. I can point the way and describe the rules of the road, but I cannot tell you everything you will encounter on your journey.

Writing an action plan will give you credibility to marshal resources and mobilize neighbors. It will give you leverage over those who only plan day to day. It will give you something to point to when you're asked, "What makes you think you can do better when so-and-so tried and failed?"

But just as with any business plan, you're not going to know all the answers off the top of your head. You're going to have to dig. You're going to have to pick up the phone and network yourself into the community to get answers. And that is why you will succeed.

You are about to learn how to unlock the innate wealth stored in inner cities. And when the concepts of LDNR start to click and you write your community-specific action plan, you will truly be able to buy low and sell high.

PART 1: THE MAP

CHAPTER 2:
THE ROADMAP

The following is a general framework that provides a lens through which you can view a typical neighborhood revitalization process.

I want to give you a detailed explanation of the roadmap's derivation because:

1. There will be times when you will feel discouraged and you'll need to find your bearings.

2. Sometimes you will feel stuck, but a clear understanding of what LDNR stage your block is in will help you pick projects that will resonate with neighbors and move you towards the next milestone.

3. You will need a reminder when it's time to switch tactics in order to make progress. Each stage has its own set of objectives. When you graduate from one to another, you need to use different tactics to reach the new objective.

4. This framework will give you an idea of how to present concepts to different audiences. For instance, if you're speaking to landlords – talk about property values. If you're talking to neighbors – talk about belongingness.

5. You will need to fight off **fear** and **doubt** to move forward in **FAITH**. Thoroughly understanding the principles herein will give you something to hold onto during times of trouble.

As previously stated, I placed the full explanation of how the Landlord-Driven Neighborhood Revitalization (LDNR) was created in Appendix 1. I encourage you to read it to improve your understanding, but building wealth is like practicing yoga. You can follow the instruction and get all the benefits without understanding the theory behind it. So, with that being said, let's dive right in with a few definitions.

DEFINITIONS

Catalytic Landlord is a rental owner who assumes a leadership position in a troubled community to quicken the pace of neighborhood revitalization.

Neighborhood Revitalization is the process of improving an area and its reputation so properties appraise at values similar to normal local markets. Just like a ship whose cargo makes it float low in the water, its normal buoyancy returns once it's unloaded. The same is true with neighborhoods. Troubled neighborhoods that carry "baggage" can be "unloaded" and restored. By restored, I mean their property values will be nearly the same as those in the "good" neighborhoods.

Gentrification vs. Neighborhood Revitalization
– Gentrification is when non-minorities flood into an area that has traditionally been occupied by minorities. The investment strategy I'm touting hinges on trying to get people from outside to come into the neighborhood. As long as honorable outsiders, regardless of what they look like, are attracted to the area, then the goal of restoring property values will be achieved.

So my version of wealth building does not attempt to dilute the population of minority residents; it focuses on improving the opinion of outsiders and eventually the opinions of property appraisers as well.

A neighborhood activist friend of mine once told me that he sees a lot of white people coming to our neighborhood now but after all the hell he's gone through he doesn't give a [care]. He says "Come on in!"

Safety – In this stage, residents may be plagued by gangs, drug dealing, poor relations with law enforcement and other issues that make the area feel unsafe. Making the area safer is the primary need during this stage. We'll discuss the process in Chapter 7.

Belongingness – In this stage, residents look for ways to connect with each other and the greater community. People are interested in establishing healthy traditions, building friendships and feeling appreciated. We'll discuss how to encourage belongingness in Chapter 8.

Title – Acquiring the title is the same as becoming the owner. The landlord is granted property rights and responsibilities along with the property deed. Tips for finding property well-suited for the LDNR are presented in Chapter 5.

Teamwork – A landlord works to join groups where neighbors, community leaders and the police/sheriff officers collaborate. The goal is to build relationships naturally and consistently over time. To advance the LDNR process, the groups must be dedicated to making the neighborhood safer. Neighborhood Crime Watch groups are ideal. See more details in Chapter 7.

Testimony - In this phase, a landlord helps people to publicly tell their success stories. They help get the word out about the community's progress and that it is no longer deserving of a bad reputation. Chapter 8 details this strategy.

I use the coordinate system to illustrate various locations along the journey.

Let me show you how it works.

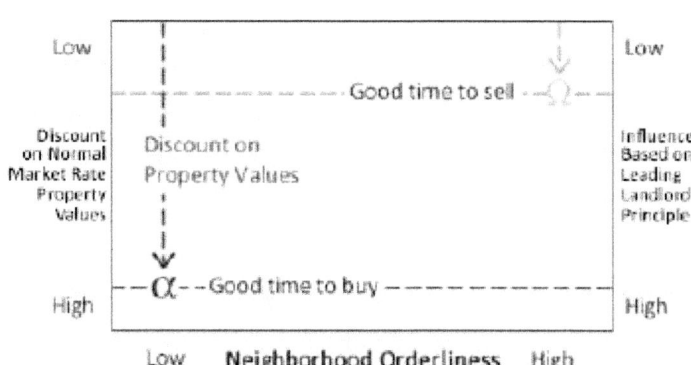

Let's make a point (that we'll call α) represent a property that is in a disorderly neighborhood (low order) that has heavily discounted property values. At this point Landlord Influence is very high because it's easy for motivated landlords to get rid of problem tenants and clean up the area.

If Warren Buffet was interested in inner-city rentals, he might buy in at this point. He typically makes a move when few are looking and/or when owners are distressed. This might be a good time for you to write an action plan and purchase as much investment property as you can handle.

The point we call Ω represents a property that has been revitalized and is now in an orderly neighborhood (high order). Notice the property values are only slightly discounted and Landlord

Influence is low because everyone is generally happy.

This is a good time to sell the properties that were acquired at point near α and capture the restored value (any appreciation you gain via rent increases would be a bonus).

Now, let's connect the points. As we do, we must draw a curve that has a noticeably flat section as it climbs. Property values improve as orderliness increases but it's not a straight shot.

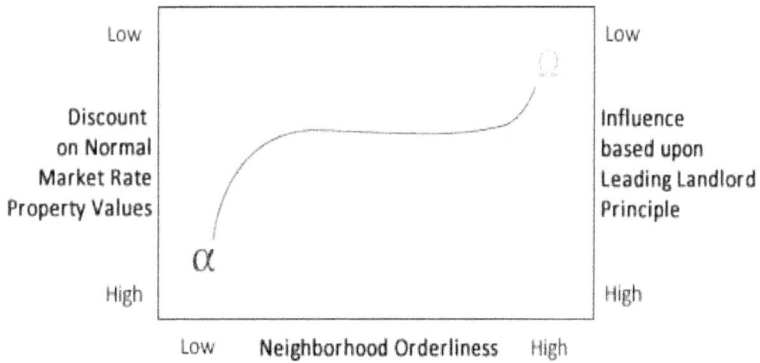

Here you see, starting from α, property value increasing as safety issues are resolved; then values flatten until the general public is willing to give the area a second look. When they do, they find evidence of the changes and become willing to form a more favorable opinion of the neighborhood.

INTRODUCING THE LDNR CHART

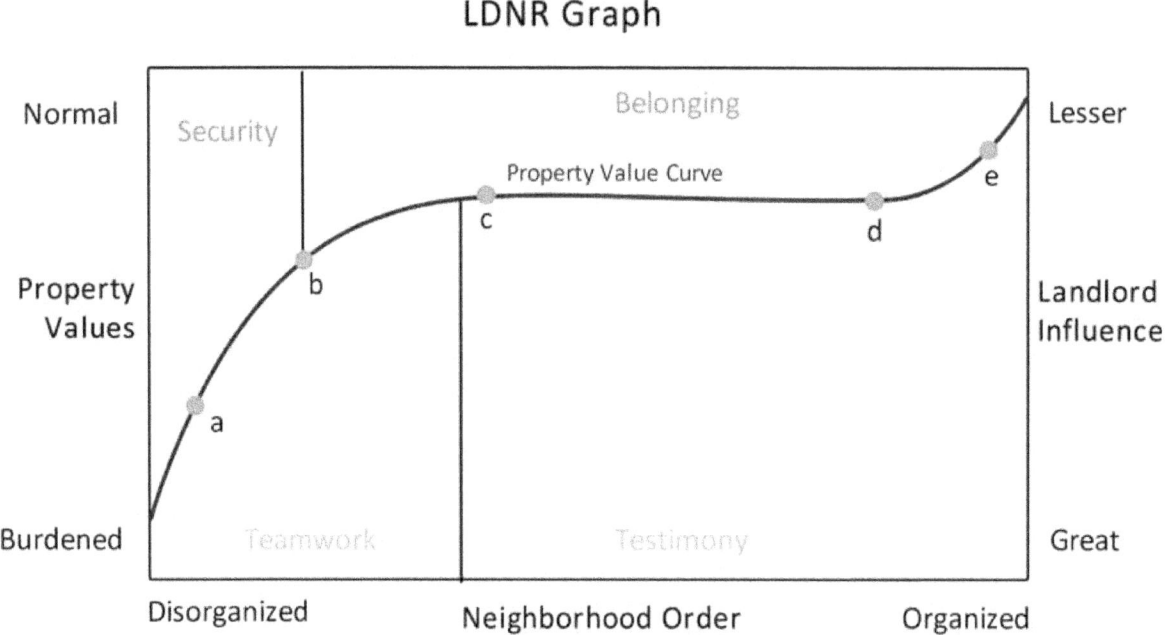

Let's pull everything together in terms of property values. As the LDNR Chart shows, values may sharply increase once safety issues are resolved, yet stagnate until the broader community considers the area to be safe. The discount remains in effect until the area's reputation improves.

We will discuss how a landlord actually uses this framework in Part 2, but for now it's important to understand that:

1. Property values increase as the discount placed on the neighborhood diminishes

2. The discount diminishes as the neighborhood becomes more orderly

3. Landlords are especially able to influence the orderliness in a troubled neighborhood

CHAPTER 3:
STAGES & STONES

Now that you understand the components of the LDNR Chart, it's time to show you how to use it.

STAGES ON THE ROAD

Just like some roads change their names when you cross a major reference point (street intersection, town hall, or body of water), the stages of neighborhood revitalization also change after major events. For the shortest, most efficient restoration possible, it is critical for local leaders to announce changes in status and the new tactics that go along with them.

There are four stages along the path to recovery, and each stage has a unique set of objectives.

Each stage also has its own set of challenges and rules. The stages are: Safety, New Norms, Lag and Catalyzed. Let's look at them one at a time.

Safety

There are a lot of unsavory activities in public view and people are on edge over their personal safety. This stage is marked by gangs, gunfire, graffiti, drug abuse and poor unity between groups. The majority of the people in this neighborhood are out for themselves and have a poor opinion of their surroundings.

During this time, optimism is rare and police are cynical. Apathy is at an all-time high. The objective here is to work as a team to neutralize safety concerns.

New Norms

The bad guys are gone and people are sorting out how to behave and adjust to the new normal. Just like with a freshly paved highway, people are confused when driving on it until the traffic cones are set up. Once lane lines are painted and boundaries are clarified, people know how to manage themselves and move along in comfort.

It's interesting to note that travelers don't care how difficult it is to get lane lines painted on asphalt. Travelers simply want to trust that someone knowledgeable was in charge of putting down the lines.

There were times after our neighborhood had adopted New Norms when a landlord would inadvertently allow a drug dealer to rent from then. This would frustrate the neighbors and really pull down moral. "Here we go again!"

In these cases I would take the lead in contacting the owner and assisting them with gathering evidence needed to file eviction. I would also remind the neighbors of how far we've come and our decision to never go backwards.

Since I didn't live in the neighborhood, I always have "fresh legs" and can pick up the baton when others start to faint. I'll expand more on this topic in Chapter 4.

During the New Norm stage, a Catalytic Landlord's objective is to model desired behaviors and work with a team to increase a sense of belongingness in the neighborhood. The stronger the new behaviors are modeled, the less you and other neighborhood leaders need to confront undesirable behaviors.

The Lag

In this stage neighbors know things have greatly improved; but unless outsiders give proper deference, the neighborhood will remain an insider's secret. People outside the neighborhood will still view the area through the frame of its previous reputation. Naturally, this affects the demand for housing and there is relatively no relief to the discount placed on property values.

At this stage, a Catalytic Landlord's objective is to launch a small public relations campaign aimed at the larger community. The campaign will help neighbors tell their 'Before and After' testimonies and increase their sense of belongingness.

It is a common practice to spread salt on icy roads to make the ice melt faster. Although there is acost for the salt, it pales in comparison to the safety and economic activity a clear road permits. In this analogy the "icy road" is the bad perception outsiders have about your neighborhood. It prevents them from coming in to do business or considering the neighborhood as a place to reside.

A Catalytic Landlord spreads the "salt" that's needed to quicken the return of economic activity. They deliberately do this to shorten the time needed to get rid of the stigma separating them from a large return on their investment.

Catalyzed

Something really good happens that gives the neighborhood its 15 minutes of fame. There's a big ribbon cutting ceremony and lots of positive news coverage that makes outsiders reconsider their opinions.

You'll know you're in the sweet spot of this stage once you see evidence that your area's property values are increasing faster than what's typical for your town. That will be because your property is experiencing a reduction in the discount along with normal appreciation. The objective in this stage is to sell off your holdings OR to switch to doing business as usual.

THE MILESTONES OF PROGRESS

You may be asking how you'll know when you've transitioned from one stage to the next. After all, there are no street signs or markers. You'll recognize the change because you will be on the lookout for some changes in attitudes and positive conversations about the neighborhood.

A milestone is like a marker placed along a road to serve as a reference point to reassure travelers they are on the right path. It can also be an important event that serves as a turning point.

I want to identify some milestones for your journey. Look for these indicators as you progress through your neighborhood revitalization process. Use these markers to modify your tactics and update your objectives.

Burn the Boat

Greek commanders used to burn their boats once they landed on an enemy's shore. This made a tremendous psychological impact on their troops – and on their enemies as well. The Greek soldiers understood victory was their only objective.

For our purposes, the same mindset is needed to ensure the neighborhood remains vigilant about restoration. Work to get neighbors dissatisfied with the status quo so the majority will tip the neighborhood forward and won't tolerate detractors. The DVP Change Formula in Chapter 10 will help you with this.

The goal is not to settle for just a safe neighborhood when you want a great neighborhood. Good is the enemy of great.

You'll know that you're making progress when there are more and more outcries for raising standards and people in general demand equality and social justice for themselves or their children. This will bring you to the Burn the Boat milestone.

Burn the Boat events are not manufactured. They usually involve a tragedy; something that throws neighbors off balance and makes them reach out to each other.

A good leader needs to have a sense of awareness to spot these opportunities and match them with solid blueprints for advancement. We'll talk more about creating those blueprints in Chapter 6.

Now, just for clarity, I'm not suggesting that you have to be the leader of every effort or speak up after every disturbing event. I am recommending that from a LDNR perspective, you should:

1. Do something to financially support leaders who are making a positive difference, and

2. Encourage other landlords to do the same

The Burn the Boat signal means it's time for your group to frequently and publicly model new behavior. In the New Norms Stage, you'll also need to confront old habits that you don't want to persist. You'll know New Norms are in place once there's a swelling of neighborhood pride.

We are the Champions

Have you ever been on a team that won a championship or overcame a large challenge together? Remember how team spirit soared? It was important to everyone in your circle but outsiders would not have a clue about your great accomplishments unless someone told them.

That's what happens in this part of the journey. It's time to shift gears. In this stage of ownership you'll find that your property value cannot increase; no matter what improvements you make or what your team achieves. It's the beginning of the Lag phase where "testimonies" are needed to persuade the larger community to take a fresh look at your neighborhood. It's time to tell your stories to outsiders.

Discovery

At this point the larger community and opinion-makers deem your neighborhood is worthy of a second look. They discover that your area is not what it used to be.

Exit

You sell your revitalized property when it's in the Catalyzed Stage or switch to doing business as usual.

With this understanding of stages and milestones in mind, let's look at the LDNR Chart again with all the layers turned on.

This should be an "Aha" moment and you should also recognize that to move from left to right, from heavily discounted to slightly discounted property values, you need to increase the orderliness of your community.

Orderliness is the name of the game – don't get distracted.

The Day Oak Park Demolished a Washington Market

This was a big day in Spring of 2007. We gathered on a Saturday morning to watch a bulldozer begin the demolition of this liquor store that had become a landmark for drug dealing and gang activity. Even though store owners had changed and the store was subjected strict anti-loitering codes, nothing seemed to curb the drug dealing and violence. As a last resort, organized and determined neighbors pressured the City of Sacramento into buying, demolishing, and reusing the site.

I wore my construction hard hat to celebrate. It was raining yet around 100 other neighbors and activist joined me in the crowd and exchanged high fives.

Neighbors who had had stray bullets fired into their homes stood in this crowd as the drug dealers in the nearby apartment complexes looked on.

A few speeches drew applause but nothing in comparison to the ground shaking cheers that went up when the backhoe's ram knocked the first hole in the wall. No matter what people thought of our neighborhood before, no one could deny that the residents had taken it back and it was not a good idea to test our will to keep it. We were organized.

So, here's the big question: "Is it possible for a landlord to intentionally increase orderliness?" Sure it is, and I bet you can already envision how you could assemble a team to do this. Therefore, yes, it is possible to make a good profit by helping neighborhoods get back on their feet. You can bank on it!

Let's get away from the graph and look at the LDNR process as a journey. I need to show the chart as a picture to give it texture; there are some important caveats I need to share with you.

The graphic to the right shows the stages and milestones fitted together to illustrate a typical neighborhood revitalization journey. For a landlord, the process starts by acquiring [A] heavily discounted properties in a troubled neighborhood, then working with neighbors to address safety issues. After an event that motivates people to become extremely dissatisfied with the status quo, it is important to:

- Introduce an improvement plan

- Hold a Burn the Boat ceremony [B]

- Begin shifting tactics to model new norms

I've introduce a loop at this stage because if you miss this "turn" and don't get enough neighbors to cross over, then you're likely to continue to face safety issues until another terrible event occurs.

"Never let crises go to waste."
— Rahm Emanuel

Once past the Burn the Boat milestone, you'll want to implement new norms. As we will discuss, it only takes a handful of behaviors to unwind the street mentality that prevents neighborhoods from unifying. We'll discuss those traits in Chapter 7.

Then neighborhood pride will begin to swell [C]. At this point a Catalytic Landlord should switch tactics to focus on public outreach. This means helping residents give their testimony that lets outsiders know the area is worthy of a fresh look.

Eventually an extremely positive synergy will occur and the community at large will recognize your neighborhood. Having been discovered [D]; there will be a sense of euphoria where the "Catalyzed" stage takes on a life of its own. It will suddenly be cool to be associated with the neighborhood. [E] This is the time to exit your investments or switch your mindset to do business as usual.

Now you can see the journey mapped out before you. Are you ready to make the trip? I sure hope so, but I need to share another piece of the puzzle first.

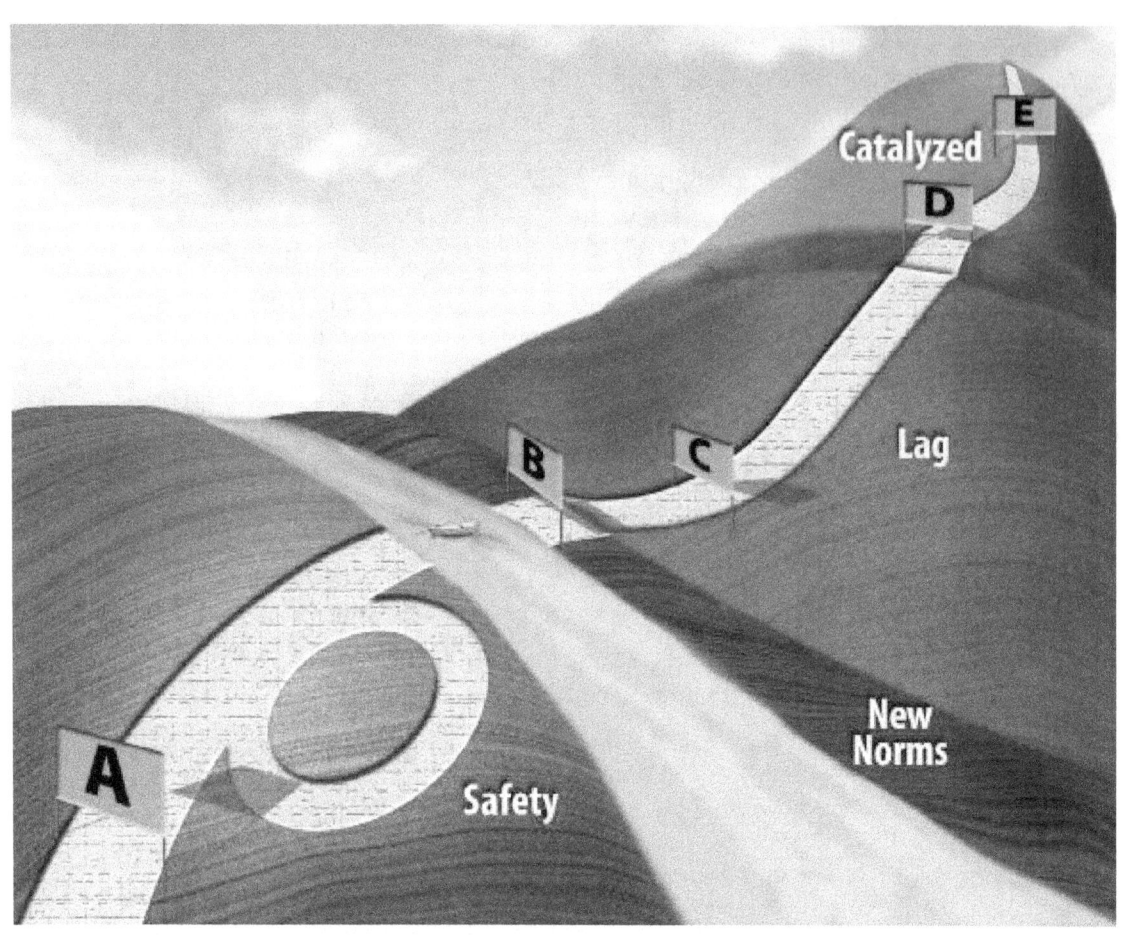

PART 2: LOGISTICS

The management of the flow of resources
between the point of origin and the final destination.

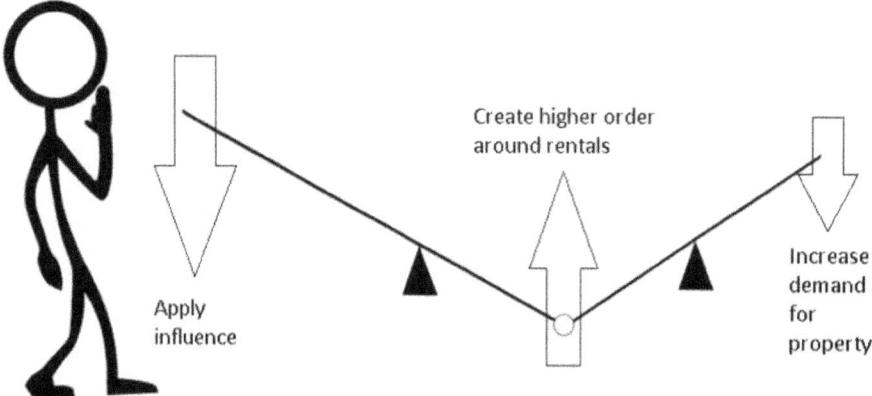

CHAPTER 4:
THE MECHANICS OF NEIGHBORHOOD REVITALIZATION

Did you know that you increase odds of making a profit every time you exert yourself on behalf of your neighbors? your reward, both financially and emotionally, will come - just at a later date.

I included this chapter to illustrate the full potential of what a non-resident landlord can do for a neighborhood. By "non-resident" I mean that the Catalytic Landlord does not reside in the actual neighborhood as it is undergoing improvement.

Let's start by looking at the connection between the Leading Landlord Principle and the Broken Window Theory. They are part of the same system. You can link them together because they both have the "High Disorder" term in common.

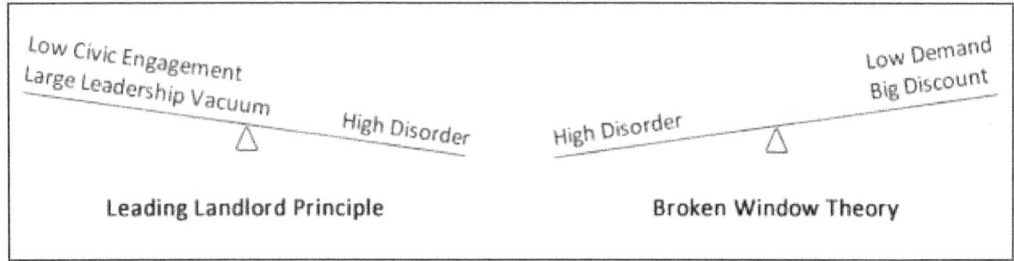

When you place a hinge between the two teeter totters, the mechanics would look like this:

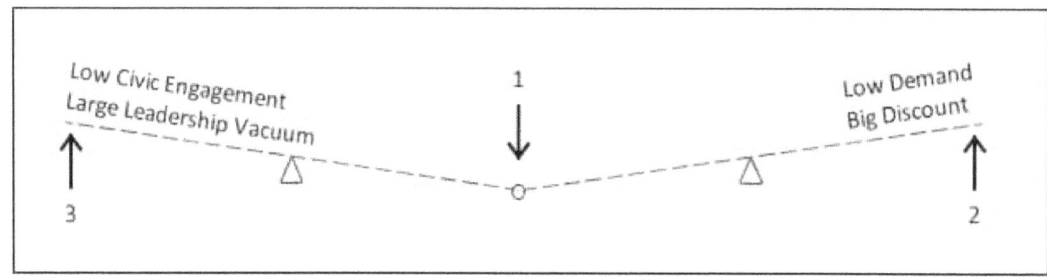

Now you can see the interconnection better. As the graphic implies, the two teeter totters link together to form a system that we'll call a contraption. The contraption first sages in the middle as disorder increases. This reduces the demand/desirability of the neighborhood and gives rise to a desperate need for an advocate to restore order.

Here's how advocate influence works: Just as a pendulum at the end of a swing wants to go back to the center; well, so does a neighborhood in disarray. Pent up energy is available to any leader that steps forward with a viable plan and a compelling vision. They can make good things happen.

Any advocate can work to reduce disorder by helping to organize the neighbors and enforcing some healthy norms. There is nothing magical about it. What's worthy of attention is how this civic engagement displaces undesirable elements and results in improved property values. NOTE: All too often advocates that do the most work are not positioned to benefit from the wealth they create by improving the neighborhood.

An advocate simply needs to use their influence to press and hold the neighborhood in a beneficial position. This means they need to do things that nudge the neighborhood in a more orderly direction and diligently stick around to make sure the changes become permanent. They champion the process of reducing disorder, hold people accountable, follow up on promises, contribute funds and demonstrate that the change is not a passing fad.

Just as the figures above imply, if the advocate lets up, the contraption will return to its former state. The advocate must stay in position until either he or she:
recruits a replacement fo a similar size and strength to do the work, or
get others to contribute just a little so the neighborhood remains orderly.

We're aiming for the latter option.

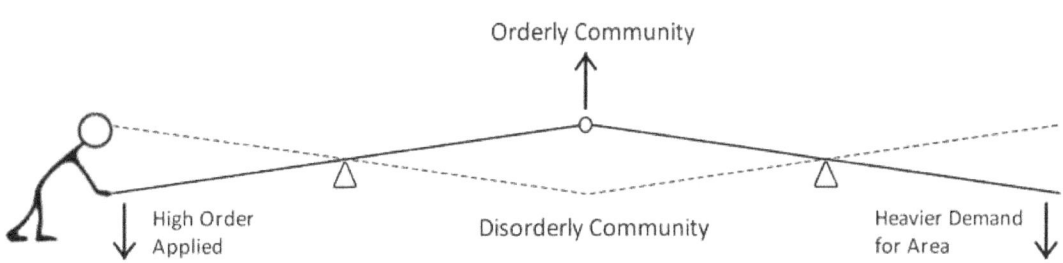

Let's look closer at the mechanics by comparing a resident advocate (that actually lives in the neighborhood) with a non-resident landlord. In the figure below, the box represents the amount of effort needed to tip and hold the neighborhood in the right direction.

As the figure implies, in troubled neighborhoods where non-owner occupancy rates are high and incomes are low, non-resident landlords have more leverage and need to expend less effort than resident advocates for the following five reasons:

Non Resident Landlords Have More Leverage than Residents

Resident Advocate
High Order Applied

Little Discount of Property

Non Resident Landlord
High Order Applied

Little Discount of Property

Landlord Leverage

1. **Celebrity Status** – they are presumed to be rich and live in a nice neighborhood.

2. **Landlord Peer Status** – an advocate landlord is better able to "bully" other landlords.

3. **Observer Status** – Renovating a home while you're living in it can wear you out. The same could be said for a neighborhood revitalization effort. Having some distance between you and your investment/renovation keeps you looking at the effort from Michael E. Gerber's E-Myth perspective. You want to work on your business and not in your business. The distance helps you focus on encouraging residents to get involved and be strategic with your revitalization efforts.

4. **Non-Resident Status** – A landlord can provide "cover" for residents who are fearful of retaliation.

5. **More Endurance** – More leverage means you can hold a position with less effort and with less fatigue. The LDNR process could take five to ten years.

DORMANT SUPER HEROES

Here is what I've been building up to say since Page 1 – inner-city landlords don't need to act like victims! Due to the five reasons listed above, non-resident landlords have more power at their disposal which gives them an extra-large amount of leverage. They are able to improve a struggling community more than anyone else. They also have a financial incentive to do so.

So then, what is the problem? The problem is that they are doing business as usual.

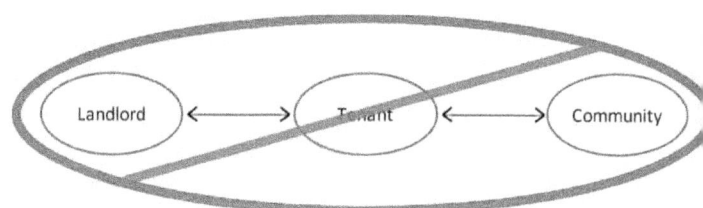

They are not engaging the community surrounding their rental and are possibly trying to be passive investors in an area that is hurt by the strategy.

As discussed in Chapter 1, doing business as usual is not effective if you are trying to mine the abundance of wealth stored in inner cities.

Using inner-city rentals as ATMs is a waste of an awesome opportunity – the opportunity to leave a neighborhood better off than when you found it.

A Matter of Honor - The Boy Scouts have a rule:

"Always leave the campground cleaner than you found it." They try to instill this sense of honor into the character of young people.

I think inner-city landlords should adopt a similar rule:

Leave the neighborhood more orderly than you found it.

Don't squander the opportunity to make a difference while making a profit.

As Professor Michael Porter suggested, entrepreneurs should lead the way to revitalize inner cities. It's in our self-interest and, in the case of the inner-city landlords, it is also well within our capabilities.

PART 3: THE JOURNEY

Vision without action is a dream.

Action without vision is simply passing the time.
Action with vision is making a positive difference.

- Joel Barker

CHAPTER 5:
ACQUIRE - STARTING OUT

Map Location: Identification of a heavily discounted property and evaluation of its LDNR potential

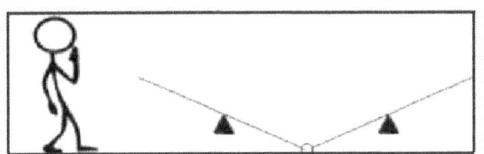

You, the investor, consider purchasing the property and estimate if you want to take the LDNR journey

Landlord's Objective	To purchase heavily discounted rental properties with as many strategic attributes as possible
Neighborhood's Objective	To survive day to day
Rules of the Road	Make sure area is suited for LDNR. (You must believe the neighborhood has potential)

The process of evaluating an investment property is largely the same whether you're in the inner city or not. The fundamentals need to pencil out; your financial projections need to make sense. However, after seeing so many people with good LDNR intentions buy property with poor post-revitalization potential, I think some pointers are needed.

As the chart above shows, heavily discounted properties are on the market and, as the stick figure shows, you are considering the purchase. This is the beginning of the LDNR process.

The goal is to evaluate the property in terms of its LDNR potential. Will it be easy to revitalize the area around the property? Will it lead to an uphill battle? Will the restored property value be worth the effort?

When I looked at my first inner-city investment I was thinking in terms of gathering enough equity to be able to retire before I was 50 years old. The discount on my eightplex, at the time of purchase, was approximately $300,000. That was a nice chunk of change at the time – it motivated me.

You should be thinking the same. Your potential payday needs to be large enough to keep you in the game when you hit a rough patch. So think big!

Following are some additional tips on attributes to look for:

NON-OBVIOUS ATTRIBUTES FOR PROFITABLE INNER-CITY INVESTMENTS

Here are five principles you should consider while selecting inner-city investments:

1. **Buy on the boundary.** Strong opportunities exist along the fringe of the "good" and "bad" neighborhoods. The goal is to profit from improving the "bad" edge and connect it to the "good" area of town. If you buy in the middle of a troubled neighborhood, in some gang stronghold, it will be that much harder to make a noticeable difference.

   Visual impact is important and can't be overstated. Your goal is to implement low cost activities to fool people into thinking the area is stronger, more organized and safer than it really is. It is much easier to portray your investment as being within the "nice" part of town if it is adjacent to or within eyesight of your ideal neighborhood.

2. **Buy into an active community group.** Future profits are directly tied to the effectiveness of a neighborhood association or grassroots advocacy group. These groups provide passion, credibility, emotional support, media connections, political influence and more. A landlord should work to grow and strengthen these groups, but not concoct one from scratch. I recommend that you attend a few Crime Watch or neighborhood meetings to help you decide on a target area. If there appears to be a functional group with passionate leadership in place, then you should short-list this neighborhood.

3. **Buy near mass transit options.** A wise strategy is to create inner-city housing that appeals to Gen Y'ers and echo-boomers. This demographic is expected to move into the inner cities over the next few years. As the cost of oil increases, so should the demand for walkable and transit-supported communities.

4. **Buy something large enough to make your efforts worthwhile.** Try to transform the largest blighted property on the block. Or pick up a cluster of homes/condos so you have a significant amount of ground under your control. You want to be viewed as a dominant player; it's much easier to work with neighboring owners from this vantage point. Just like anywhere else, purchasing the right property in the right location goes a long way towards ensuring a profitable investment. So look for great deals with these attributes and set yourself up for a success story.

5. **Buy near landlords who have similar revitalization intents.** The Napa Valley wine industry has been successful partly because a lot of wineries have clustered in the area. By clustering together the area, the wineries are able to make an impression, and that attracts talent and supportive businesses. Do the same with your rental business. Buy close to others that are interested in revitalization and help them build momentum.

Key Question for Your Action Plan

- Where is the boundary of your target neighborhood revitalization?

- What are the strengths, weaknesses, opportunities and threats of your target properties within that area?

- Are there groups in position to assist you with revitalization efforts?

C H A P T E R 6:
ASSUMING A LEADERSHIP ROLE — STARTING OUT

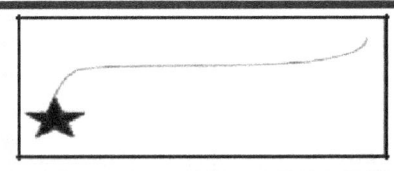

Map Location: Accepting the Call

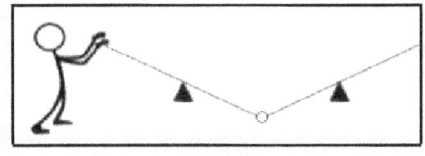

The stick figure shows the investor has decided to engage the community and play the role of a Catalytic Landlord

Landlord's Objective

To make a go/no go decision on becoming a Catalytic Landlord

Neighborhood's Objective

Same as before – nothing has changed. The objective is to continue to survive

Rules of the Road

- Become a model landlord
- Create a physical equivalent of your decision to work to revitalize the area
- Introduce yourself to the community

Many inner-city real estate owners understand their property rights but fail to accept the obligations that go along with them. It's easy for them to see an area which desperately needs more leadership but it never occurs to them that they are the missing leaders.

In this chapter, we'll take a closer look at the things you should consider before deciding to become a Catalytic Landlord.

At this point, the goal is to get off to a good start, build credibility and begin to create the momentum needed to overcome the large obstacles that weigh down your property values.

MAKING THE DECISION — IS LDNR STRATEGY RIGHT FOR YOU?

Let me be the first to point out that this strategy is not the best choice for every investor or for every inner-city area. It is not a one-size-fits-all remedy. In fact, the opposite is true; the stars must align.

Here's how to evaluate if you should not become a Catalytic Landlord.

Do not become a Catalytic Landlord if:

1. You do not think highly of the local police officers or believe they will be trustworthy partners in efforts to restore the neighborhood.

2. There isn't a watch group or advocacy group in your target area. After all, your goal is to accelerate revitalization, not to start from scratch.

3. You're unable to purchase a large cluster of residential units or influence the largest landlord in the area.

4. You do not have long-term interest in the area.

5. The majority of housing is owner-occupied. You only can gain the upper hand if the majority of residents are renters.

There may be more conditions, but basically, if you are not bullish on the area then you should not attempt a full blown LDNR investment strategy as a Catalytic Landlord.

If you don't believe the neighborhood will eventually turn itself around, then you shouldn't become a Catalytic Landlord. Pretty straight forward, right?

But there's more. Let's look at you. Do you have the desire to become a neighborhood leader? Are you willing to:

1. Grow as a person and develop your leadership ability?

2. Make weekly inspections on your holdings for the next five years?

3. Grow as a public speaker and become a spokesperson for your block?

4. Accept the role of a tribe leader?

If not, then becoming a Catalytic Landlord may not be the best choice for you.

Did I scare you off? It's OK if I did. You should probably move on to a different type of investment strategy to help you meet your financial goals. That's fine. Now, if you're still reading this, I'm going to spend the rest of this book writing as if you're cut out for this journey.

THE MINDSET

What are you signing up for? What's the job description? I used the term "catalytic" (even though some think it's too nerdy) because it perfectly describes the investment mindset. All we need to do is modify the chemical definition with financial terms and the role comes to life.

Catalytic Landlords use their capitalistic desires to fuel their charitable efforts aimed at shortening the time needed to revitalize a neighborhood.

If you believe time is money, then you'll intuitively understand that reducing the time to achieve your investment objectives is simply good business.

Inner cities suffer from a lack of effective leadership. Illegally dumped furniture and debris stays on the streets far too long because no one reports it. Eyesores such as graffiti and litter remain in place way too long because no one insists that it be removed. Even though it may not cost anything to get these problems resolved, residents typically shrug their shoulders, cope and wait for someone else to do something. I call this the "no snitching" mindset.

Accepting the role of Catalytic Landlord means you accept the role of tribe leader. You become the squeaky wheel that gets the grease for your block. If you see something wrong, then you make a call or send the note and track the action item through to completion. It will also be your job to break down the "no snitching" mindset by encouraging others to take a "We're all in this together" mindset. More on this is in Chapter 7.

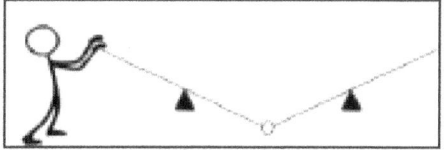

Congratulations if you've decided to move forward as a Catalytic Landlord! Please let us know about your decision. We want to send you inspirational stories and encourage you on your journey.

Go to www.CatalyticLandlord.com **and tell us who you are.**

THE FIRST 90 DAYS

The process of becoming a Catalytic Landlord can begin at any time. Just because you didn't start off as a Catalytic Landlord doesn't disqualify you from taking up the role. If your neighborhood is in disarray, then there's still an opening for a "leader." It's uncontested, too.

CHARACTERISTICS OF A CATALYST	CHARACTERISTICS OF A CATALYTIC LANDLORD
Participates in a reaction that is going to occur. A catalyst accelerates what is already in motion.	Redevelopment funds must already be committed or a stimulus project already underway before you take position.
Participates in smaller portions relative to the overall reaction. For example, there may be 1 part catalyst for every 100 parts of other components.	The investor leverages the work of others to bring about increased property values. Like a CEO, the investor inspires, empowers and assists more than actually performing all the work.
Is not harmed by the reaction.	This is not like the civil rights movement. You should not put yourself at risk to accelerate the neighborhood's restoration. Safety first.

Here are some things you should consider during your first 90 days:

1. Craft a good 8-second introduction. It may sound something like, "Hello, I want to reach out and introduce myself. I'm Al Williamson and my property is right next to yours. I think we could make the street safer if we knew each other. What do you think?" NOTE: If

   you don't speak the same language as your neighbors, find someone to translate. The extra effort will pay huge dividends as your campaign progresses.

2. Touch base with your rental nearly every day for 30 days – learn what is going on and increase your exposure. Drop in at random times so you can observe conditions throughout the day and night.

3. Take on a front yard curb appeal project. Let there be a physical equivalent to your decision to become a Catalytic Landlord. People need to see something different at your property.

4. Make an effort to introduce yourself to the owner of every property (which may not be the residents) that surrounds your holdings. This means getting their tax billing information, creating a directory, sending them a card or giving them a call. Find a way to contact them before there's an urgent need.

5. POWER MOVE Shut up! Listen, listen, and listen some more. During the first 90 days, try to learn other people's hopes and dreams. Get to know as many people as you can and learn what they're passionate about.

Don't talk about your plans or this catalytic stuff. Don't say or do anything to imply you're their saving grace. And, for God's sake, don't say anything about wanting to increase property values. Focus on listening as you meet people farther and farther away from your holdings. Do your best to suspend judgment of everyone you meet. If your neighborhood is anything like most, then things will not be as they first seem – you'll need a little time to sort the real players from the fakes.

Another reason to suspend judgment is because inner cities typically have a high concentration of people with mental illnesses. You will need these people, as well as everybody else, as you advance your campaign. So seek out their dreams and strengths as well – don't overlook them.

THE UNDERLYING KEY ASSUMPTION

Before moving ahead, let me state that this investment strategy assumes you're not a hypocrite. It assumes you're operating as a model landlord. Your property holdings will come under scrutiny once you raise your profile and start demanding higher standards. So make sure you keep your house in order.

Once my wife and I took ownership of our 8-unit apartment, our first order of business was to empty out the place. The previous owner had allowed the complex to become a hub for drug dealing and prostitution. It sorely needed a reboot.

We made the tenants an offer they couldn't refuse; we offered them $500 to move within 30 days. We also provided them with rental listings and moving boxes. Maybe we went overboard, but all but one were out before the deadline.

At the time, $500 was enough to help them place a deposit on another apartment and since they didn't have any savings, $500 would have prevented them from moving. So we basically removed the chalk block on their wheels.

This little deposit refund maneuver brought about benefits such as:

- Avoiding eviction expenses.

- Giving tenants with poor payment histories a fresh start.

- Eliminating the cat and mouse game of trying to control drug dealing/prostitution-related traffic on my property.

However, the biggest benefit of the reboot was that neighbors were relieved the chaos was gone and treated us as heroes. In 30 days we had accomplished what the police and politicians had been unable to do for years… we helped neighbors get a peaceful night's sleep!

POWER MOVE: It is very likely that the tenants you inherit will have a do-everything-for-me mindset. This is typical of people at the bottom of our economy.

It will be your goal as tribe leader to follow the example of Dr. Mimi Silbert of the Delancey Street Foundation to weaken this dependency mindset. (More on Delancey Street in Chapter 7.) Once people see your commitment and accept your leadership, you will be able to show them that everyone has something to contribute. First demonstrate that you'll sink or swim with them and then expect them to help with the neighborhood's restoration.

Key Question for Your Action Plan

- *How will you deal with the tenants you inherit?*

C H A P T E R 7:
MOVING FORWARD – TEAM BUILDING STAGE

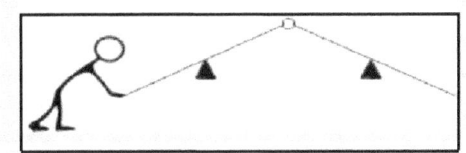

Map Location: The discount will decrease as safety issues are resolved and fewer distressed owners are willing to sell their properties at any cost.

Here the Catalytic Landlord is playing a major role in the community and waiting for others to join in.

Landlord's Objective	• Apply influence to do things residents are reluctant to do. • Assist groups that advance the community's safety. • Model New Norms for others to emulate.
Neighborhood's Objective	• Build/enlarge teams to improve community • Discourage undesirable behavior.
Rules of the Road	Help break street culture by building trust between neighbors.

As documented in Influencer: *The Power to Change Anything*, by Kerry Patterson, if you change just a few high-leverage behaviors then large, unsolvable problems can get resolved. Whether it's preventing guinea worm outbreaks, fighting the battle of the bulge or reducing neighborhood crime; focusing on just a few highly effective habits makes all the difference.

I worked with Mr. Ibrahim Hughes of We Buy NJ Real Estate, LLC in Union, NJ, to identify eight habits of highly effective inner-city landlords. The habits can be grouped into habits for the team building phase and habits for the lag phase.

As discussed at the end of Chapter 3, this first stage is the safety stage, where property values are heavily discounted due to the lack of demand. The community is in disarray, has a poor reputation, its formal and informal groups don't share resources or collaborate, and few would choose to live there if they had other options. At this stage, the Catalytic Landlord begins practicing simple, but high-leverage habits known to reduce crime.

HABITS FOR REDUCING NEIGHBORHOOD CRIME AND INCREASING SAFETY

At this stage a Catalytic Landlord should join teams of residents that work on safety issues and cooperate with authorities to reduce crime. The mission is to build upon small successes; learn to work together and create an atmosphere that repels crime.

Practice the following habits, in sequence, to build goodwill and get off to a great start.

Habit 1. Respect Your 'Hood

Simply being an inner-city landlord grants you a little celebrity – use that and show esteem toward others. Activate the Law of Reciprocity by showing respect to everyone, especially those whose behavior you don't like.

Let's be clear, this is a campaign. It's up to you to initiate acts of unmerited respect to advance your cause.

Be aware of the "code of the streets" that many inner-city residents abide by. Treating them with respect will help them accept your leadership and follow your lead.

Not "losing face" and maintaining respect is critical in many cultures; but the way loss of respect is handled varies greatly. In some cultures, people feel it's appropriate to kill themselves if they face great shame. The street culture leads one to seek revenge on whoever caused the shame. This may explain why you hear of fights breaking out because someone looked at another person the wrong way. Respect is everything to people who feel that every day is a struggle for survival.

Anyway, not to drift too far off our LDNR topic, I just want to emphasize that you must be sensitive to the issue of respect. Do this by:

1. Initiating a humble self-introduction.

2. Initiate showing respect first by granting people the deference they want (not what they might justly deserve).

3. Make it safe for people to talk to you by granting them an abundance of dignity.

Behave as a political candidate running for office. After all, you are running a campaign. Go out of your way to show respect to all homeless and young people you meet. Make them your allies.

Habit 2. Show Up After Something Bad Happens

There are reasons why presidents visit disaster zones; it comforts those needing a sense of order. The inner-city landlord who checks on her tenants and neighbors after something bad happens will garner goodwill and exponentially boost her celebrity status. Also, this act of kindness directly helps a landlord's bottom line through lower vacancies, higher net operating incomes and earning the loyalty of neighbors.

If you heard there was an act of violence or robbery in the area, you should reach out and express concern. If someone's car gets broken into, contact them and ask how you can help them recover. That's how you rebuild a neighborhood.

> People don't care how much you know until they know how much you care.
>
> -Dr. John Maxwell

You don't need to rush to the scene like a TV reporter, but you do need to make a gesture to help people recover. Help them clean up and rebuild. Insert yourself and be a model for what neighbors should be doing for each other. As a best practice, try to step in and do something small that people can't do for themselves.

There is always emotional scarring that must be addressed. Specialize in healing emotional scars on your block when possible.

Simply model what good neighbors do for each other.

Build awareness for strategically helping people recover. This will help your group build the trust that's needed to move to higher levels of cooperation and gives you more goodwill to do more difficult things down the line.

If you exercise leadership during bad times, people will be more apt to follow you during good ones.

The first two habits (Respect and Show Up) help you build the momentum needed to accomplish the next three habits. You're building your influence and doing what Stephen Covey calls, "Sharpening Your Saw". That's why these two habits are listed first.

In 2006, a fellow activist had a Molotov cocktail thrown at her home. A drug dealer was retaliating against her efforts to squeeze him out of the neighborhood. Fortunately, he was a terrible bomb maker; the device didn't cause much damage.

He was also a bad judge of who to bully because the attack had the wrong effect. Instead of scaring her into silence, the act caused neighbors to rally and get involved in her effort to clean up the streets. It was a Burn the Boat act.

Several weeks after the attack, I drove by and noticed markings were still on her home's siding. I realized she must be under emotional strain. So after asking permission, a friend and I washed her siding clean.

It was a small gesture that only took us a few minutes, but it built community. It helped her recover.

Habit 3. Fight Disorder Within and Beyond Your Property Lines

Disorder is a catchphrase for graffiti, blight and litter. It creates an atmosphere that encourages illegal activities. Just as a store owner inside a shopping mall wouldn't tolerate disorder in the mall; you shouldn't tolerate it on your block. The neighborhood's appearance is your business; don't settle for anything less than the best.

Now, as a Catalytic Landlord, you'll want to be especially vigilant to fight disorder on your front lines which are immediately in front of, on both sides and across the street from your holdings. Doing so leads to the following benefits:

Activates the Law of Reciprocity - This law states that you must give first, and then the recipient feels obliged to return the favor. This is an especially powerful force in lower-end communities. A Catalytic Landlord needs the help of his neighbors. Doing simple things like picking up in front of someone else's place helps you build a reservoir of goodwill that you will eventually need to draw from.

> **POWER MOVE:** When your neighbor thanks you for picking up in front of their place, be sure to respond, "You're welcome. I know you'd do the same for me." Drive home the expectation that you expect them to have your back.

Restores Order and Makes Your Block Safer - Blight, especially lingering blight, encourages petty crime. Crooks do their business in areas where nobody cares and nobody is looking. A lack of litter and weed-free areas indicate someone is watching and someone cares. Reducing petty crime reduces the likelihood of more serious crimes, and that's good for business.

Quickens Lease-Ups - When faced with a vacancy, you want to find a replacement tenant as soon as possible. You don't want someone canceling their appointment for a showing because they changed their mind after seeing your neighborhood. Litter and blight make honorable people feel uncomfortable; so if you want to quickly attract honorable tenants, then work to create a culture that doesn't tolerate blight.

Improves Tenant Retention – No doubt about it, your tenants are affected by blight. It subconsciously affects their mood and opinion of the owner (even if they are litter-bugs themselves). Showing a clean streetscape helps meet their need to feel appreciated.

Improves the Quality of Your Tenant Profile Over Time – Honorable tenants are attracted to orderly environments. Litter and blight are repellents – so implement a blight management campaign for the long haul.

I am not suggesting that you spend all day picking up litter. I am suggesting that you must be seen picking up litter AND you must figure out how to deputize, pay or bribe others to help keep the street clean.

One of the first things I did while working at St. HOPE was to promote a neighborhood cleanup; we spent a couple of hours on the second Saturday of each month picking up litter at the park and throughout the neighborhood. My research showed that nearly every successful grassroots neighborhood revitalization effort began with a neighborhood cleanup; and I'm not one to reinvent the wheel.

This project gained momentum as local high school students came out to help (and

fulfilled their community service requirements that helped get them into college). The city supported the effort by dropping off trailers to haul away all the trash bags we filled. The local business association sponsored the event by buying litter pickers, bags, gloves and lunch for the helpers.

I ran the program from behind the scenes to encourage others to make it their own. This is how I discovered the power of being an undercover operative.

Just as with many groups; egos get in the way of productivity. I've come to realize that it's best for a Catalytic Landlord to help others stand

in the spotlight and support them like crazy so they don't fail. Their success creates your wealth. Don't forget that.

This habit of fighting disorder beyond your property lines may at times cause you to spend some of the goodwill that you've built up with Habits 1 and 2, but that's OK. Goodwill should be spent to achieve strategic objectives; and upgrading the standard of what's acceptable is the most important objective in the safety stage.

Right off the bat you want to do something easy and get an easy win. Create a success that you can build on.

You may find that some owners simply aren't aware of the disorder issues. Some may only visit their rentals no more than once a month or only as needed. They may not know their fence was tagged or that their night lighting is burned out. And even if they did see these issues, they may not be aware of the consequences of not quickly restoring order.

So bring these issues to your fellow owner's attention. It's a mutual cash flow and safety threat that should not be ignored.

I once interviewed a visual pollution technician who applies a wax-like coating to structures that are routinely tagged. After the bridge or street sign gets tagged with graffiti, the owner simply power washes it off then reapplies the wax coating.

The tech said that taggers eventually give up because their "art", which may take hours to create at great personal risk, gets washed away before anyone can admire it.

He went on to say that once competing taggers see a rival's tag, they feel compelled to tag over it like "a dog marking a tree." The original taggers then feel disrespected and have to redeem themselves. They go back to retag with an even larger display of graffiti. And thus the cycle repeats.

The tech said he tells people that graffiti tags are like weeds – it's easier to take care of them early on.

Obviously, graffiti and blight are things you don't want, but what are the things you do want?

Your neighborhood revitalization campaign depends on getting the visual cues right. Just as you decorate your house to usher in holiday cheer – you should set up visual cues to create a crime-intolerant atmosphere. These cues will affect everyone's thinking (consciously and subconsciously), which will affect their behaviors, and eventually affect your property values.

DO THIS: Begin creating and installing visual crime determents. The benefits include:

1. Giving the bad guys will get the hint and move to a less organized area.

2. Indirectly fighting crime. It's safe, non-confrontational and...

3. Helping people see a glimpse of the neighborhood's potential.

Visual Deterents for Landlords in Tough Neighborhoods

- Police cars on patrol.

- Neighbors chatting with police officers in the middle of the street.
- Top speed when removing graffiti from buildings and fences.
- Lots of public greetings and open communications.
- Neighborhood Watch signs.

- "Smile, You're on Camera" signs.

- Litter-free streets.

- Signs of neighbors cooperating and coordinating with each other.

- Great night lighting (thank God for LED bulbs!).

- Well-maintained front yards – no weeds.

- Acknowledgment of your neighbors by saying good morning, hello and good evening.

The work of piling up visual deterrents is equivalent to dropping dye in a bucket. Each drop leads to the final drop that changes everything.

Habit 4. Harness and Then Use the Collective Voice of Owners

Disorder flourishes when property owners don't communicate or pool their resources. It is easier than ever to collect the names of all the owners on your block. Just check your city's tax records or work with a real estate agent. If you practice the first three habits (Respect, Show Up and Fight Disorder), owner information will be practically given to you.

Use a moderated Facebook group, Yahoo group or social media feed. Make technology work for you. Do what Kevin Dickson did in Overland Park near Denver, Colorado, and manage the neighborhood's email newsletter list.

Persuade the group to organize around the mission of keeping the neighborhood safe, clean and attractive. This way your block can gain a collective voice that gets the ear of politicians, the police and the press.

Some effective ways to use the collective voice are to:

1. Rally when you want a drug dealer evicted.

2. Write letters on the groups' behalf (but get their input before sending it).

3. Bolster resident-run Crime Watch groups.

When confronting wayward owners: A good paradigm to work from is that other landlords are busy and aren't paying attention – it's not that they don't care. Appeal to their self-interest. Show them the financial rewards of falling in line.

When confronting wayward individuals: Frame your approach as: all of us have an issue; not with you, but with your behavior. Let them know your group welcomes them to stay – but not their behavior. Help them understand it is futile to ignore the wave of change.

Once you've perfected your use of the collective voice, you may likely find that your problems have gone away. But be prepared for challenges. Chaos will sneak back in if you don't remain vigilant.

HABITS FOR INSTILLING NEW NORMS

When you get enough people that are fed up with craziness and ready to take action, then you want to have a Burn the Boat event. The bigger and more public this event is, the better. The closer to your rental's front door, the better.

At this point you'll be able to drive out enough of the really bad actors to give yourself a chance. But once the void opens, leaders need to quickly fill it by modeling how people should behave.

Do more things out in the open, speak to each other and walk around and greet each other. People will catch on, confidence will rise, and soon you'll be on the next level singing Queen's 1970 anthem, We Are the Champions.

Inspiration from San Francisco's Delancey Street

When it comes to the subject of instilling new norms, the best place to look for examples is Delancey Street. In 1971, Dr. Mimi Silbert and John Maher started what's now known as the Delancey Street Foundation, a program that helps ex-felons, drug addicts and prostitutes. They stress self-reliance and run their programs without government assistance, without a formal staff and without social workers.

The foundation operates more than 12 for-profit businesses to fund their $24 million annual budget. As of 2012, Delancey Street has graduated more than 18,000 people, many of whom have gone on to become lawyers, doctors, teachers and other contributors to society.

They clearly have a handle on how to break down the street culture that holds so many people back. The Delancey Street Foundation is also living proof that no one is beyond help.

The following page contains excerpts from an interview with Dr. Silbert where she talks about how they break the street culture and instill new norms:

"We take the people everybody else thinks are losers... our only criteria is that they want to change badly enough."

"My job is to be the chief believer, to believe in them when they don't believe in themselves..."

"...And I say to them at the beginning... We're climbing a mountain together. I'm at the top of the mountain. The newest person is at the door at the bottom. But we're holding hands. So if all of you are pulling downward, we'll all go down together. If all of us pull upward, we'll all go up together. But we're hanging in together..."

"It isn't enough in life to just take care of yourself. Life isn't just about you."

The fundamental philosophy at Delancey Street is simple: A helps B and A gets well.

"You've got to teach them how to interact, how to get up out of their ghetto mentality and into the mainstream, how to deal with every race, every ethnic group, every kind of person with every skill."

With these lessons from Delancey Street in your head, I suggest you follow this next habit to help your neighborhood advance during the New Norm stage.

The Power of Organized Landlords

I once asked unruly neighboring tenants to turn down their music – I was about to do an apartment showing and wanted to make a good first impression. They refused – so I politely commented that I didn't have a problem with them, but with their landlord – and walked away. The indigent young man was wise enough to know that we were organized and that I just might have his landlord's number on speed dial – so the music was quickly turned off. The tenant also moved out a few months later (which might just have been a coincidence – but maybe not).

This is an example of allowing someone to save face while restoring order. May you use it in good health!

Habit 5. Be a Landlord's Landlord

Encourage other landlords to fall in line. You, as a fellow landlord, may be in the best position to influence other landlords. Some ways to do this are:

1. Initiate contact with surrounding landlords to inform them of issues that affect their investment.

2. Collect donations for common interest fundraisers.

3. Be a conduit to help busy landlords get involved.

4. Share resources and news – who doesn't need to know a highly

5. recommended handyman?

6. **POWER MOVE:** Create a Landlord's Association for your area. Help landlords communicate and resolve issues that would otherwise go unaddressed. The ability to tell a fellow landlord some of her outside light bulbs need to be replaced is a simple act, but prevents an unattractive nuisance that may lead to more serious issues.

Having landlord-to-landlord conversations that focus on financial self-interest is one of the most powerful things you can do to improve your neighborhood.

Recently I saw an apartment, similar to my own, that had several units boarded up. This property housed the last remaining "issues" for our area and had been the subject of a police raid. I decided to reach out to the apartment owner to offer my sympathy and assistance.

I teamed with some fellow landlords, one of whom is a real estate agent, and found out the name and address of the new owners, who happened to live hundreds of miles away. Then I drafted a letter, had my team members tweak it, and second-day mailed it to get the owner's attention.

Here's what the letter said:

> *Hello Mr. _____:*
>
> *My name is Al Williamson. For the past 10 years I've own and managed the eight-unit apartment complex that's around the corner from your property at _____, Sacramento, CA.*
>
> *My building used to be the most problematic property in North Oak Park, but now it is very much under control.*
>
> *If you're interested, I would like to share with you some Oak Park specific practices that may help you operate your complex easier and more profitably.*
>
> *Please give me a call or send me an email at your convenience. I look forward to working with you to increase both our property values."*

If I don't hear from the owner, I'll send a couple of follow-up letters with photos of the current state of the property and specific requests for the owner to address. And if those efforts don't bear fruit, I'll get our local code enforcement involved.

The process is very straightforward and doesn't really require much effort. I simply copy a method that has worked for others, and now I'm just following a 'best business practice' that's worked in the past. Just another day at the office.

THE SEQUENCE

If you haven't guessed already, these habits need to be applied in order to be effective. They build on each other to push the level of orderliness forward and they help you build momentum. This is a step-by-step process that you implement over time. But be warned, your chance of building a team might diminish if you skip a habit or do them out of order.

CHAPTER 8

MOVING FORWARD – MINIMIZING THE LAG

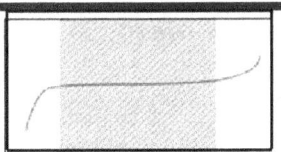

Map Location: This is the Lag Stage where people have more conversations about belongingness.

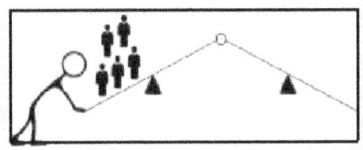

Here the Catalytic Landlord is joined by residents who see the benefits of insisting that the neighborhood remain orderly.

Landlord's Objective

- Continue adding to visual crime deterrents.
- Plant lots of information you want your potential buyer to discover.
- Help residents tell their "Before and After" stories.

Neighborhood's Objective

Continue to strengthen a sense of belonging by supporting cultural celebrations and other community events.

Rules of the Road

While neighbors don't mind their neighborhood being a hidden gem, landlords and business owners should team up to promote the neighborhood.

Let's continue the discussion on getting others to help you raise your property values. At this point in the journey, your neighborhood is doing fine but still gets no respect.

As the figure shows, in this section of the chart, orderliness can nearly double before there's any significant increase in property values (discount shrinkage). It's an excellent time for residents but a frustrating one for landlords who are looking for

equity growth. The stick figure shows that residents are becoming more involved, and less effort is required of the landlord.

The area still has problems but they are under control. The majority of people outside the neighborhood still consider it to be

questionable and unappealing. As with any transformation, there is always a lag before the new creation is clearly observable.

During the lag stage, the Catalytic Landlord must shift into high gear. It is time to spread salt on that icy road! It's time to help outsiders realize your area deserves a fresh look. This is the stage where you focus on promoting good news and encouraging others to get on the bandwagon. But all along, you should plant clues for your future buyer to discover. There's a two-fold benefit to this work; to move forward you must see signs that others are embracing the new norms and feel good about shifting your focus to address brand management.

HABITS TO REDUCE THE LAG TIME

Habit 6. Support Annual Community-Building Traditions

Local events, especially block parties with ice breaker activities, give neighbors an excellent excuse to meet each other. The benefits include:

1. Crime-proofing the neighborhood by promoting unity and neighborhood pride.

2. Giving other landlords and local businesses the opportunity to show goodwill and make donations.

3. Increasing tenant satisfaction and lowering vacancy rates.

Be sure to find ways to associate your holdings with these events. It may be that you play a sponsorship role or maybe just serve on a planning committee, but do something to make the event worthy of your larger community's attention. Think big and challenge the outsider's perception of the neighborhood. You also want to choose events that create a sense of belongingness and neighborhood pride. For example, assuming all things were equal, I would rather support a Fourth of July party over an Easter Egg Hunt. The Fourth of July has a civic pride element associated with it. Get it?

Let me say again for emphasis, it's not necessary for you to lead all these projects. But it is necessary for you to financially support (with very small donations) strategic projects and work to see that they grow. Just like a CEO, work to help others improve your stock.

National Night Out

There are two grassroots programs that guarantee a Catalytic Landlord's success: Neighborhood Watch and National Night Out. When crime prevention groups come together to celebrate National Night Out, neighborhood rejuvenation is just around the corner. Most people are aware of the Neighborhood Watch program which began in 1972. Their 'one-eyed' street signs are well-known crime deterrents. According to the National Sheriff's Association, the program is effective because it breaks the link between crime and social disorganization. You can bank on crime rates dropping when neighbors start talking to each other.

The lesser known program, National Night Out, began in 1984 and is growing in popularity. This annual event, held on the first Tuesday in August, encourages people to meet their neighbors. According to the National Town Watch website, in 2012 over 37.5 million people in 15,700 communities held ice cream socials, potlucks and block parties on that day. Naturally, this generates momentum for Neighborhood Watch programs, and that is why both programs work together, like bicycle pedals, to move neighborhoods forward.

I've attended the National Night Out block party near my apartment building since 2008, but in 2010 we decided to organize one in front of our eightplex. We typically have 75 – 100 neighbors attending, along with police officers, our city council representative and the mayor. We've been hosting the event ever since.

As a best practice, we ask our neighboring landlords to contribute $30 each so we can put on a nice event. Although the event is potluck, we like to have nicely decorated areas and lots of door prizes. We use the prizes to "bribe" people into participating in our ice-breakers and fun contests.

Specifically, we had contest for who was the longest and newest term resident, who knew what Washington Market was, who knew the most people, who was the fastest, etc. These games were both a history lesson and an orientation for new residents.

We also use some of the landlord-donated money to get our local businesses involved. For example, if we buy a $10 gift card from a business, we ask them to match our gift. This way we leverage our seed donations and walk away with two to three times as many gift cards and plenty of supplies.

All of this benefits landlords in a tangible way – leading to bigger parties and an upward spiral!

Habit 7. Promote and Circulate Good News

Similar to blight and disorder, good news also has a snowball effect. During the Lag, you want to deliberately spread good news about your neighborhood to those OUTSIDE the neighborhood to:

1. Attract businesses which create new jobs.

2. Give tastemakers and trend-setters the new information needed to form new opinions about your area.

3. Encourage the residents and community leaders – there's nothing like seeing your event on the local TV news or newspaper.

I want to stress here that your motive should be to always get good news out to your future buyers and build demand for your properties.

The press is always looking for material, so send out short press releases to help them. Try to quantify your success (how many people attend, how many trash bags were collected, or the amount of money donated).

This makes it easy for reporters to write about you. Find out who is compiling a list of the top 10 neighborhoods and start courting them.

Figure out who is the trendsetter in the larger community; give them some insider information and see if you can get them to say something positive about your community. Yes, this is a campaign, so campaign smart.

Habit 8. Support Local Reputable Businesses

Encourage residents to support local businesses that cater to them. Simultaneously, use the power of your collective voice to reduce the density of non-reputable businesses (liquor stores, massage parlors, etc.) that bring neighborhoods down. For example, if neighbors want nicer restaurants in the area, then make sure they are supporting the ones you currently have. Encourage your existing restaurants to donate to neighborhood meetings and support revitalization efforts. Working to make your local businesses successful is the best way to attract more businesses and more jobs! Here are five practical things a landlord can do to support local businesses:

1. Go out of your way to bring outsiders in to see the 'best-kept secret'.

2. Give away gift cards for local businesses.

3. Find ways to incorporate local businesses into community discussions; connect the job makers to their potential customers.

4. YELP about them or submit online reviews

5. POWER MOVE: Give gift cards to Crime Watch groups to use as door prizes and incentives

KEY TAKE AWAY – A landlord has an opportunity to influence the time the area is in the Lag phase by working to improve outsiders' perceptions. It's in a Catalytic Landlord's self-interest to purchase and spread the "salt" that melts the icy relationship between the formerly troubled neighborhood and the larger community.

When successful, your efforts will help attract businesses and spur a renaissance that leads people to become interested in the community again. This, of course, will enlarge your pool of potential applicants and reduce the discount placed on your own property – thus increasing property values.

Does all of this sound like too much work? Is it overwhelming? If you're thinking those thoughts, like I used to, I want to encourage you to look at the situation from a CEO's perspective. The job of a CEO is to equip and empower those who will increase profits. They are always predicting returns on investments and taking actions accordingly; and this should be your mindset as well.

In a *New York Times* article, *How a Detroit Landlord Made His Properties Hot*, Melina Emerson describes how Eric Brown of Urbane Apartments uses two habits to create excitement about the area surrounding his rentals. The result is that he can charge a premium and has lifted his own property values.

He uses Habit 7, Promote and Circulate Good News, as he talks up what's cool about his neighborhood via his blog. He doesn't passively wait for the 5 o'clock news to sprinkle in a nice story. Instead, he blogs about the area and glamorizes the "apartment experience".

I especially like his quote about how his blog talks about everything except his apartments. It shows me he really understands that in social networking, direct hard sales don't work. Pointing out what's cool and getting others to comment on what's cool, is the best approach.

Brown also uses Habit 8, Support Local Reputable Businesses, as he talks up local restaurants, services and activities. But hang on; it looks like he also draws advertisement revenue from these local businesses as well. Wow! He's getting paid to do something that ends up helping his own property values. How smart is that?!

Key "Minimizing the Lag Stage" Questions for Your Action Plan:

- *Who are the entities that you could collaborate with to help you makeover your neighborhood's image?*

- *Is National Night Out celebrated in your neighborhood? Could you assist or sponsor the event on your block?*

- *Who, in your local press, should you contact and start building a relationship with?*

CHAPTER 9:
FINISHING THE JOURNEY

Map Location: This is the post catalyzed stage where property values rise in line with values in the "good" neighborhoods.

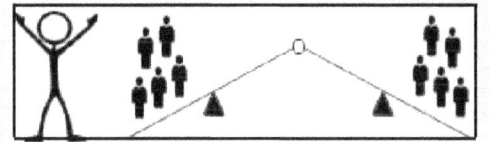

Outsiders start enjoying what the neighborhood has to offer and further increase demand without the Catalytic Landlord's involvement.

	• Increase rents.
Landlord's Objective	• Improve tenant profile as much as possible.
	• Sell holdings during the euphoria - market upturn.
	• Do business as usual going forward.
Neighborhood's Objective	Build upon success.
Rules of the Road	Catalytic Landlords should switch to doing business as usual.

The final stage of neighborhood revitalization is when the real fun begins. In the "Catalyzed" stage it's time for business as usual; which is well covered in other real estate books.

As the chart shows, this is the time when property values are unburdened and rise to normal market levels. The stick figure shows that residents have engaged. They are filling the leadership vacuum and keeping order in the community. Eventually someone will take notice and make a large investment into the community, and that will change how outsiders view your neighborhood. The interest from outsiders will further increase demand and the Catalytic Landlord no longer needs to actively participate in the image makeover campaign.

The increased demand might translate into the ability to increase rents, but for our strategy we are banking on improved property values resulting from improved public perceptions.

There should be a nice increase in your property values and you should consider selling and collecting your reward. However, it may also be time to keep your properties, lay down your sword and shield, and reap the benefits of your efforts. In either case, let me remind you again of your ultimate goal of LDNR in the figure shown below.

The goal is for the landlord to switch places with the tenants and for the residents to support their community in a positive way. Now that the community has momentum, the landlord doesn't need to play a central role.

Working yourself out of a job is a nice way to finish strong.

It's hard to imagine a restored neighborhood ever fully reaching the same value as the nearby "nice" neighborhood, but it could come close.

Now, if you plan to sell, make sure you don't sell prematurely. It takes more than decision-makers giving the area a nod of approval. Look for new buildings, new businesses, or other financial factors that compensate for the former stigma – signs that an appraiser can point to as evidence that your neighborhood has completed the restoration.

> ### Key "Finishing the Journey" Questions for Your Action Plan:
>
> - *How will you operate so you can exit smoothly?*
>
> - *What area of your neighborhood do you expect the improvement to come from?*

PART 4: TOOLS FOR YOUR TRIP

The good fighters of old first put themselves beyond the possibility of defeat, and then waited for an opportunity of defeating the enemy.

To secure ourselves against defeat lies in our own hands, but the opportunity of defeating the enemy is provided by the enemy himself.

- Sun Tzu, The Art of War

CHAPTER 10:
FIGHTING THE RESISTANCE

Now that you know how to read the map and how to make an efficient journey, you need to know you're going to hit some bumps along the way. Road conditions change as you move from one stage to the next; and the path is not always smooth.

In this chapter, I want to share three tactics to help you deal with the turbulence you should expect. They are:

1. Develop a Thick Skin

2. Hold & Take Ground

3. Dissatisfaction-Vision-Plan Change Formula

These tactics will help you create a sense of inevitability and will weaken the opposition's will to resist restoration efforts.

The LDNR strategy is directly linked to your abilities as a leader. Your investment will get better as you get better. I've listed some additional resources

in Chapter 12 and in the workbook at www. CatalyticLandlord.com to enhance your leadership skills and make people more inclined to follow your lead.

Don't Be Surprised By Resistance

For every action there is an equal and opposite reaction. And when it comes to moving a neighborhood out of equilibrium and spurring on improvements, you can bet you'll face an opposite reaction. You should not take this personally. Everyone who has tried to lead a group to a higher state has faced resistance.

This is why it's so important to practice the 8 Habits in sequence. You need to first create a reservoir of goodwill which you can then spend as needed to achieve your mission.

The Resistance –What is it?

The Resistance takes on many forms. It may come from your tenants who don't possess a positive vision for their future, and see your work as something that will lead to rent increases. It may come from outside forces such as local drug dealers, gangs, taggers, litter bugs, street-walking prostitutes and/ or non-cooperative landlords. Surprisingly, it can also take the shape of local activists fighting against gentrification.

The Resistance is mostly made up of those terrified of change and those engaged in illegal activities; they won't welcome your attempts to improve the status quo. Don't be surprised by this – and don't spend any energy trying to convert people. Just be successful and displace them instead.

But there is some good news. The Resistance is made up of the vocal minority. The silent majority is hoping you won't back out of the fight.

Restoring a neighborhood's intrinsic value is a noble and moral investment strategy. Residents deserve to live in a safe and clean environment. So make no mistake, this is a worthy battle to take on. And you're getting a head start by reading this book.

Your goal is to tip public perception in your favor and make the Resistance fight an uphill battle until they quit and give up.

What the Resistance is Not

The Resistance is not composed of everyone who doesn't see eye to eye with you. Expect to encounter many diverse opinions – after all, the lack of a common vision is one reason the neighborhood fell into disarray. It is not particularly helpful to label the people you wish to partner with, "the Resistance." Their opinion is just as valid as yours; and you should hope the largest and most defined ideas will prevail.

FIGHTING THE RESISTANCE ALONG THE JOURNEY

You will naturally fight the Resistance by persistently using best practices; such as the 8 Habits of Highly Effective Inner-City Landlords. It's a type of martial art for landlords.

The Habits will help you build momentum and easily overcome some of the more petty problems that cause division.

Fighting the Resistance is not beyond your skill set; you don't need specialized training. You do, however, have to learn to develop a thick skin.

Thick skin; the ability to be misunderstood without quitting, is an absolutely vital trait to master; and something you can learn along your journey. If you don't, the Resistance will sideline you and take you out of the game.

THICK SKIN – YOUR DEFENSE AGAINST JAGGED EDGES

Any time that you engage a community you open yourself up to being misunderstood. In fact, people will go out of their way to find offences or to twist your words.

When you lose "frame control," your elementary school memories of being teased will come rushing back as some sharp-witted, washed-up 'comedian' belittles your efforts. The harpooning will sting. If you're making progress, you're going to face criticism. It goes with the territory.

Here's where you'll need to remind yourself to focus on the weight of your actions, not your momentary popularity. Take things in stride like other public figures do. Hopefully, your potential financial reward is large enough to get you past this dip.

Some things to remember:

1. Know your motive – know why you're in the game.

2. Reframe the attack – keep it in perspective – not everyone in the world believes the bad press.

3. Don't take yourself too seriously – after all you're not without faults.

4. Work first to build good will so there are plenty of visible successes that should speak for you.

5.

"Always forgive your enemies; nothing annoys them so much."

– Oscar Wilde

Whatever you do, don't let a hard patch sideline you. Don't let it make you quit your campaign. Just speak less and act more.

HOLDING AND GAINING GROUND

Now, whereas I'm not a fan of war, I am a fan of war strategy; especially when it comes to advancing a campaign to make a community more attractive to job creators. And since this book is about using best practices to liberate inner-city wealth, I need to point out that Sun Tzu wrote on this topic. His thoughts have stood the test of time for centuries.

I suggested in Chapter 5 that you buy on the edge of the inner city and advance out from there. This is a form of expanding your campaign from a strong position. Sun Tzu points out in the *Art of War* that you must not lose ground. Don't give up territory. Instead, you take a little ground at a time and save it (incorporate it) and take a little more.

Now by "take a little ground" I'm talking about expanding the area that contributes to your revitalization efforts – expanding the area that looks orderly and feels safe.

Sun Tzu writes in the *Art of War* that you cannot create opportunities. You must realize that opportunities are all around you and learn to see them.

Work on the easy things, secure them, and then work on the next sure thing. Fill the voids with an attitude of 'better days ahead', teamwork and neighborhood pride.

You are, in a way, waiting for the enemies to reveal their weaknesses, such as a strained relationship between foes, or a new common enemy you can fight against. Take every opportunity to build trust, and parlay that into neighborhood restoration.

The simple act of meeting more people and recruiting them to the cause helps you gain ground. Every person that joins your campaign increases the orderliness in the community. **Allow the Resistance to provide you with opportunities to defeat it.**

Sun Tzu also advises you to put yourself in a position where you cannot be defeated. I take this to mean not to branch out into risky positions and don't embark on projects that have little chance of success. It means not walking the streets alone at midnight or putting your safety at risk. That is not the way of a Catalytic Landlord; you must not compromise your personal safety. News of you becoming a victim might set back your revitalization efforts for years.

This is the way to build momentum without making big mistakes. As Sun Tzu points out, your defeat is within your hands; don't overreach. **Don't provide opportunities for defeat.**

THE DVP STRATEGIC CHANGE FORMULA

Dissatisfaction is always in ample supply. Wouldn't you like to use it as fuel to move your neighborhood forward? Well, you can.

Since the mid-80s, political and business consultants have used versions of this conceptual model to help organizations transition to higher levels. And you too can have the same success if you understand that sufficient amounts of each change element are needed to topple the status quo. Those elements are:

- **Dissatisfaction** – answers the "Why?" question and fuels the change effort.

- **Vision** – answers the "What?" question and must be compelling enough to entice action.

- **Plan** – answers the "How?" question and it must be a blueprint forward, a treasure map.

This model is commonly known as the DVP Change Formula.

If one of these elements is missing, then you're heading towards failure. There won't be enough weight to tip the scale and not enough steam to make it over the hill.

This formula is especially useful when dealing with shortsighted people who resist efforts to improve the neighborhood.

The Resistance doesn't work from a plan, nor do they have a goal that inspires people. So keep this in mind. Those that oppose improvements are playing tug-of-war while standing on marbles. They hope they can scare you off and make you quit.

Don't let any media attention fool you, either. The media likes to give both sides of every story. Unfortunately, this misrepresents the number of people that share each point of view. Be prepared for your opposition to get their share of airtime regardless of their level of sophistication. Don't let that unsettle you.

The Catalytic Landlord that understands the DVP model has a significant advantage over the Resistance. You're able to both engineer a civic movement and, more preferably, troubleshoot a struggling revitalization effort.

> "Dissatisfaction and discouragement are not caused by the absence of things but the absence of vision."
>
> – Anonymous

Use the DVP Formula to Attract What You Want

The DVP Formula is a tool that can help landlords bring about positive change. Use it to gently remind people how unhappy they are with the status quo. Be illustrative with your vision, show pictures if you can. Help people travel into the future and give them a glimpse of how the neighborhood could be if they shared your vision. Then talk about the steps in your blueprint for going forward. This is how you create a wave to wash away the elements that oppose neighborhood revitalization.

Say you want neighboring landlords and owners to work together to make your block nicer. You should:

1. Talk about how it's unfair that your block doesn't have what another block does (D)

2. Talk up or illustrate what your block would look like if it had "what it deserves" (V)

3. Share a written plan that details what steps to take next to advance your cause (P)

Do things in this order and you'll increase your chance of making a change?

Use the DVP Formula to Repel What You Don't Want

While managing the Guild Theater, I constantly needed to chase away panhandlers. If I didn't, we wouldn't be able to break the stereotype that haunted our community (and substantiated the

So, after making sure the panhandlers knew where they could find a meal and other social services, I would use a script that followed this outline:

1. We need more jobs in this part of town (D)

2. The event we're hosting could help us attract more jobs if we're successful (V)

3. We need you to leave so you won't obstruct the effort (P)

This approach was very effective and, like a good politician, I used it all the time when I needed to make something happen.

Now that you know the formula, you'll see it used in every political speech that tries to topple an incumbent. Use it to attract elements that your community needs and to repel those it doesn't.

C H A P T E R 11:
PUTTING IT ALL TOGETHER

Let's review our central thesis one final time. If I were going to preach about the LDNR strategy, I would outline my sermon like this:

THESIS – BREAK OUT	TRAITS AND NUISANCES
Landlords in troubled communities	• Low income • High crime issues
Can increase their cash flow	• Reduce their vacancy rates • Charge higher rents • Reduce repairs related to poor quality tenants
Increase their property values	• Reduce the discount on values (negative premiums) • Broken Window Theory
Increase the quality of applicants	• Create an atmosphere that attracts honorable people • Repel unproductive behaviors
Increase the quality of applicants	• Assuming advocate role • Leading Landlord Principle
By improving the orderliness of the community surrounding their rental	• Use team-building tactics to build safety • Use testimonial tactics to build public image

I'm hopeful that all of this rings true to you. Throughout this book, I've tried to lay out a process where you could nod in agreement at each step. Each step should have seemed logical and customizable for your community.

If that is the case, then this investment strategy should be something you can bank on. Entrepreneurs, as Dr. Michael Porter says, can lead revitalization efforts for inner-city communitites. And since Delancey Street's Mimi Silbert tells her ex-felons that "A helps B and A gets well," I believe she would tell inner-city landlords that if they help their community they will prosper.

The following graphic shows that when landlords engage the inner-city community surrounding their real estate holdings, they can increase orderliness and bring about a movement that increases their property's value.

#1 Acquire an inner-city property that's strategically positioned for a successful revitilization campaign.

#2 Landlord assumes a leadership role and begins applying influence.

#3 Landlord acts as a catalyst to do things residents are reluctant to do. This gives residents a glimpse of the neighborhood's potential.

#4 Residents get onboard a bandwagon of success.

#5 Landlord exits after developments justify an increase in demand and outsiders show interest.

#6 Community moves forward as residents and outsiders advance their mutual self-interests.

So let's revisit the original central question: What makes you different from others who have tried to revitalize the area and failed? The difference is in the following six reasons:

1. You'll use a grassroots approach for restoring one block at a time.

2. You understand how to align yourself with other owners for a self-sustaining, self-interested approach toward restoration.

3. You will use an action plan that focuses on behaviors that are well within a landlord's control and that have proven to be effective elsewhere.

4. You understand the change process and know what's needed to improve the odds of leading a group to a higher level of orderliness. You also understand how to prevent others from undoing the progress.

5. You're anticipating the Lag phase and know of ways to minimize it without losing ground.

6. You've anticipated Resistance and have plans to outmaneuver it.

Yes, you deserve to be considered as a credible force. You are now 1000% more prepared than I was when I started my map-less journey.

However, I do recommend that you read the books listed in the following reference section. They will better prepare you to fight the Resistance and write your action plan.

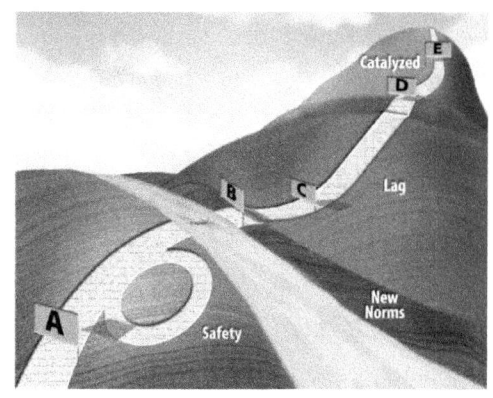

NEXT STEPS TO GETTING STARTED

As I've mentioned throughout this book, you really need to write an action plan before attempting a full blown LDNR investment. And I wrote this book to help you think through the objectives of each stage. So now you have everything you need to write an effective plan.

However, if you want additional assistance, then I would love to help. I created a workbook which will guide you through the process of creating an action plan. The workbook:

1. Prompts you with questions to get you thinking and anticipating events that may not currently exist.

2. Lists potential answers on how others have responded to challenges.

3. Helps you build awareness which will give you leverage over the Resistance.

CHAPTER 12:
REFERENCES

Crucial Conversations Tools for Talking When Stakes Are High, 2nd edition

(Aug 19, 2011) by Kerry Patterson, Joseph Grenny, Ron McMillan and Al Switzler.

Influencer: The Power to Change Anything (Sept 13, 2007) by Kerry Patterson, Joseph Grenny, David Maxfield and Ron McMillan.

The Competitive Advantage of the Inner City (1995) by Michael E. Porter.

The 5 Levels of Leadership: Proven Steps to Maximize Your Potential (Oct 4, 2001) by John C. Maxwell.

A P P E N D I X:
ONE

HOW THE LANDLORD-DRIVEN NEIGHBORHOOD REVITALIZATION CHART WAS CREATED?

Let's start off with the definitions of the concepts that are merged into the Landlord-Driven Neighborhood Revitalization (LDNR) Chart.

Defining the Zones

Human Needs Change as Lower Needs are Satisfied

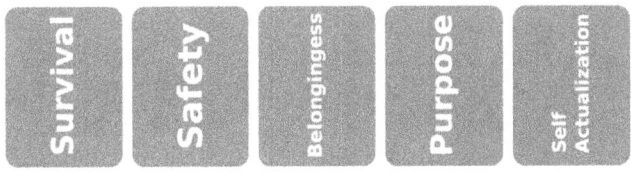

Low Order of Sophistication ▷ ▷ ▷ ▷ ▷ ▷ ▷ ▷ High Order of Sophistication

Maslow's Hierarchy of Needs - This hierarchy is a framework of human desire. You likely learned about it while in high school. It has five levels: survival, safety, belonging, purpose and self-actualization.

Each level must be adequately satisfied before advancing to a higher level; and levels cannot be skipped. For example, if a community is struggling with a crime spree (Safety) they will be too scared to attend a Fourth of July block party (Belonging).

For our purposes, we'll only consider the Safety and Belonging stages of Maslow's Hierarchy.

Safety – In this stage, residents may be plagued by gangs, drug dealing, poor relations with law enforcement and other issues that make the area feel unsafe. Making the area safer is the primary need during this stage. We'll discuss the process in Chapter 7.

Belongingness – In this stage, residents look for ways to connect with each other and the greater community. People are interested in establishing healthy traditions, building friendships and feeling appreciated. We'll discuss how to encourage belongingness in Chapter 8.

Again, let me point out that according to Maslow's rule, a person or group can only advance to the belongingness stage after safety issues are sufficiently under control.

Five Levels of Leadership - The regions in this chart are loosely based on Dr. John Maxwell's explanation about why people follow leaders during various stages of an organization's growth. Maxwell has written more than 60 books, primarily focused on leadership. He's my go-to author when I need leadership inspiration.

In his book, The Five Levels of Leadership, Maxwell says a leader has five levels of progression: title, teamwork, testimony, training and treasure. But in our model, we only use three of Maxwell's levels: title, teamwork and testimony.

The key point is that a leader (or Catalytic Landlord) needs to use different leadership techniques at different times in order to move a group forward.

Title – Acquiring the title is the same as becoming the owner. The landlord is granted property rights and responsibilities along with the property deed.

Tips for finding property well-suited for the LDNR are presented in Chapter 5.

Leadership Level Changes and Organization Order Increases

Low Order of Leadership & Teamwork ▷ ▷ ▷ ▷ ▷ ▷ ▷ ▷ High Order of Leadership & Teamwork

Real estate is all about hyper local factors. Expect leaders on each block to be on a different level of leadership with each resident AND expect each block to be on a different level of Maslow's Hierarchy. To best connect with people, it's important that you become skilled at diagnosing where they are on the LDNR map.

Teamwork – A landlord works to join groups where neighbors, community leaders and the police/sheriff officers collaborate. The goal is to build relationships naturally and consistently over time. To advance the LDNR process, the groups must be dedicated to making the neighborhood safer. Neighborhood Crime Watch groups are ideal. See more details in Chapter 7.

Testimony - In this phase, a landlord helps people to publicly tell their success stories. They help get the word out about the community's progress and that it is no longer deserving of a bad reputation. Chapter 8 details this strategy.

DEFINING THE AXISES

An axis is a reference that helps you measure something – it's similar to a ruler. It's used to compare values that are getting bigger or smaller, or attributes that are getting better or worse.

The Broken Window Theory (Left Side Axis)

In 1982, Wilson and Kelling published the Broken Window Theory which claims that crime can be discouraged by reducing disorder. Taking care of little things to reduce disorder is a guiding principle for Disneyland, Times Square and countless luxury hotels. It is, without question, what landlords should do.

"Disorder" is a general term for litter, graffiti, drug-dealing, not enforcing rules, overgrown lawns, dilapidated homes, etc. Disorder makes people feel uncomfortable. It poisons the atmosphere for

productivity and chases away honorable tenants. The less disorder you see, the better.

Taking care of the little (extremely affordable) things, such as picking up litter, helps prevent larger problems from occurring. As many case

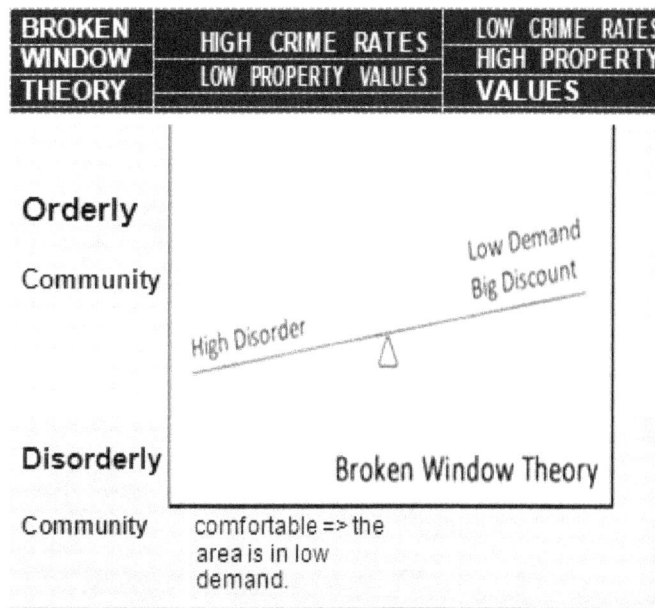

studies have concluded, reducing disorder will tip a troubled neighborhood towards restoration. Here's a look at the Broken Window Theory in matrix form:

I'll use a teeter totter to illustrate how the Broken Windows Theory works. Instead of talking about inverse proportions, I'll simply state that increasing disorder encourages unproductive behaviors and ultimately results in discounted property values.

The Leading Landlord Principle (Right Side Axis)

Here's a typical scenario: A neighborhood takes a turn for the worse; homeowners flee and rent their homes if they can't sell them. The number of renters soon outnumbers the number of owners and, by default, leaves landlords as the biggest stakeholders.

In this situation landlords hold most of the influence in the neighborhood. The opposite is true as well; a landlord's influence is weakest in wealthy and orderly communities that have few renters. I call this phenomenon the Leading Landlord Principle. It says that a landlord's ability to improve a neighborhood is greatest when the community is at its worse. This principle is presented in matrix form below:

THE LEADING LANDLORD PRINCIPLE	HIGH OWNER OCCUPANCY RATES HIGH INCOME NEIGHBORHOOD	LOW OWNER OCCUPANCY RATES LOW INCOME NEIGHBORHOOD
Orderly Community	Landlords are not esteemed Landlord Influence is Low	
Disorderly Community		Landlord are esteemed Landlord

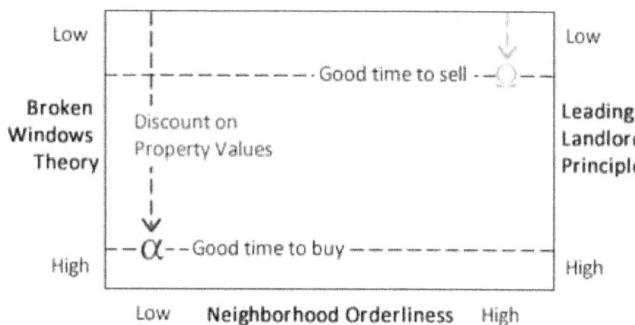

Leading Landlord Principle

To the right is the chart with all the axises shown:

Let me show you how it works. Let's make a point (that we'll call α) represent a property that is in a disorderly neighborhood (low order) that has heavily discounted property values. At this point Landlord Influence is very high because it's easy for motivated landlords to get rid of problem tenants and clean up the area.

The point we call Ω represents a property that has been revitalized and is now in an orderly neighborhood (high order). Notice the property values are only slightly discounted and Landlord

Influence is low because everyone is generally happy.

This is a good time to sell the properties that

the restored value (any appreciation you gain via rent increases would be a bonus).

Now, let's connect the points. As we do, we must draw a curve that has a noticeably flat section as it climbs. Property values improve as orderliness increases but it's not a straight shot.

This figure shows the relationship between Disorder and Landlord Influence displayed on a teeter totter.

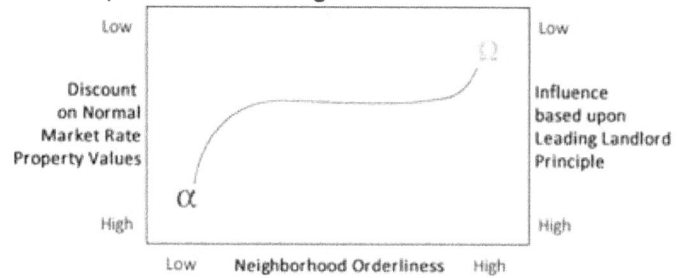

Here you see, starting from α, property value increasing as safety issues are resolved; then values flatten until the general public is willing to give the area a second look. When they do, they find evidence of the changes and become willing to form a more favorable opinion of the neighborhood.

INTRODUCING THE LDNR CHART

Let's pull everything together in terms of property values. As the LDNR Chart shows, values may sharply increase once safety issues are resolved, yet stagnate until the broader community considers the area to be safe. The discount remains in effect until the area's reputation improves. We will discuss how a landlord actually uses this framework in Part 2, but for now it's important to understand that:

- Property values increase as the discount placed on the neighborhood diminishes

- The discount diminishes as the neighborhood becomes more orderly

- Landlords are especially able to influence the orderliness in a troubled neighborhood

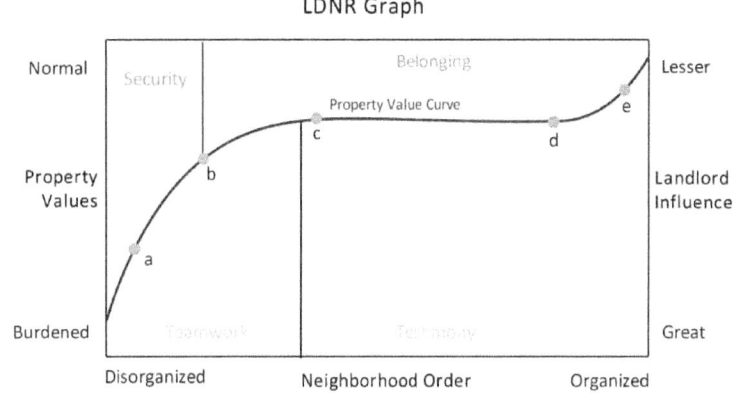

LDNR Graph

Leading Landlord™
presents

THE CATALYTIC LANDLORD

WORKBOOK

Send questions and comments to al@LeadingLandlord.com **Let's work together to create an action plan for you!**

Table of Contents

1 – Creating Your Advantage

This workbook will guide you through the process of creating an action plan by helping you spell out your vision and define the steps to take in order to bring that vision into reality. Preparing a plan will give you a more credible take on the task of leading your neighborhood through an upward transition. It should help you with gathering additional funds, partners and team members. And it will definitely give you an edge to outmaneuver the Resistance.

One of the biggest advantages of preparing an action plan is that it helps you to build awareness. I believe the awareness you'll gain will breed a sense of confidence within you … and expressing confidence will make people more apt to follow your lead.

All this results in a quicker, cleaner and more efficient neighborhood revitalization. Which, of course, is great for the residents and awesome for you, the property owner, who stands to gain equity as property values increase.

Planning isn't the most enjoyable way to spend a day and I do realize that you may not have all the answers right now, but you should press on anyway. I encourage you to do your best to answer each question and add more detail as your way becomes clearer. Your plan will give you:

1. A placeholder for critical information that you'll need along your journey.

2. A means to leverage the experiences of others who have successfully revitalized neighborhoods.

Maybe others have tried and failed at revitalizing your target area. And you'll eventually be asked why you think *you* can do better. My deep desire is that you'll be able to point to your action plan – that you're about to create - as the difference maker.

Let's get started!

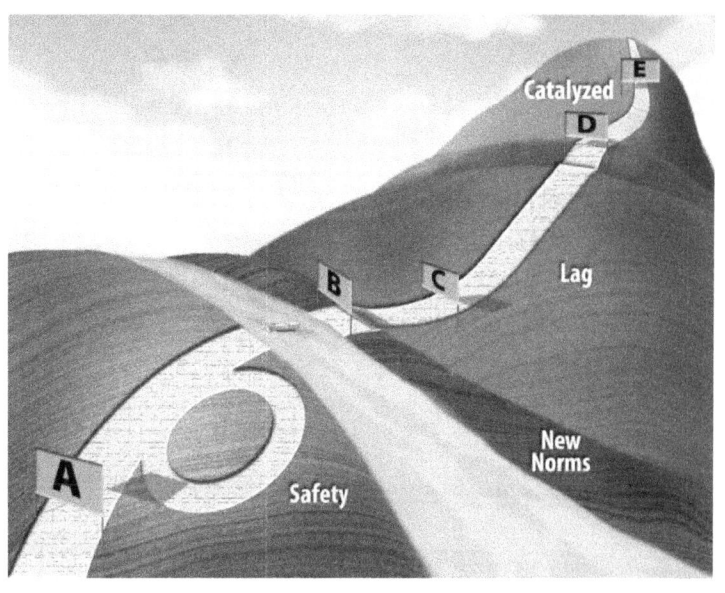

Chapter	You want to...	So you can...
5	Buy smart	Position yourself to financially benefit from the value you will create by advocating for the neighborhood.[A]
7	Strengthen teams that work on safety issues	Have enough people committed to security and intolerance of crime [B](Burn the Boat).
7	Help instill new norms	Help residents understand how to behave in a foreign land – a safe neighborhood. This will be a new sensation for many of them. [New Norms]
8	Minimize the lag	Help outsiders understand that the area has outgrown its problems and is now the land of opportunities (low rents, good infrastructure, accessibility, etc.).[Discover]
9	Help residents take leadership roles	Collect your reward by: • Relinquishing your leadership roles • Maximizing your rents • Doing business as a usual (which include selling your holdings) [Exit]

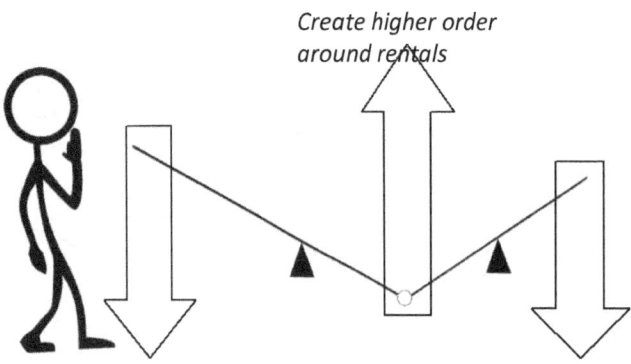

Create higher order
around rentals

Apply influence

Increase demand
for property

Make A Smart Acquisition	
Objectives	Find a rental with the as many post-revitalization attributes as possible
Attributes	1. Buy on the edge 2. Be the largest landlord or be able to influence the largest landlord in the area 3. Buy into a crime watch or neighborhood association area 4. Buy near transit options

Compare the discounted value of the property you're considering with a compatible one in a normal (good) area. The difference in price will be the prize you stand to capture once your area is revitalized.

Write this number down here: $_____. Let it quietly inspire you.

DO THIS:

1. On a map, draw in the edges of your target area.

2. Draw in the boundary of the good and bad sections of town.

3. Overlay mass transit features.

4. Overlay boundary of nearest redevelopment zone.

5. Plot the meeting locations of the nearest coffee house. Where do people gather to socialize?

6. Is there a neighborhood association or crime watch group nearby?

7. Where are the properties of the largest landlord located?

8. Is the property you're considering located near the border of your target area?

9. Mark the area surrounding the property you're interested in as far as terms of owner-occupied or renter-occupied goes. Do you think there are vastly more renters than owners?

Things to Consider

Do not proceed with a Landlord-Driven Neighborhood Revitalization strategy if:	If you're willing to work really hard, then proceed if:
The property you're considering is not close to the edge of the good and bad neighborhoods.	A crime watch group or neighborhood association is not already in existence.
You're not confident the police will be supportive of your revitalization efforts.	There are more owners occupants than renters. Having more renters in the area give you the upper hand.
You're not confident you can influence the largest landlord in the area to join your revitalization campaign.	

Use this "Five Why" exercise; it helps you to understand your true motivations and to problem solve. It is a generally accepted maxim that five iterations is sufficient to get to a root cause of an issue you're trying to clarify. Let's use it to better understand why you, personally, want to take this journey. You have a greater chance of being successful on this long journey if you have a purpose that inspires your inner being and is aligned with your self-interests.

When you hit a tough patch, you're going to be happy that you have a statement to look back on and rekindle your fire.

The "Five Whys" Technique to Help You Flush Out True Motives/Root Causes	
1. So why do you want to get involved in neighborhood revitalization?	
2. Why do you want to do that?	
3. No tell me, specifically … what's your motive?	
4. Ok, but why?	
5. Ok, but say it really succinctly and don't worry about sounding selfish. Why do you want to do this?	

Be sure to sign up at www.CatalyticLandlord.com and let us know you're taking this journey. We want to encourage you along the way and share our stories.

5 – Improving the Team

Safety – Team Building		
Summary	Your plan to introduce yourself to the community and build goodwill.	
Objectives	• Apply influence to get things done • Assist groups to advance safety issues • Model norms you want to strengthen	
Habits to Practice	Habit 1 – Respect your hood Habit 2 - Show up after bad things happen Habit 3 - Fight disorder Habit 4 – Harness the collective voice	
Success Milestones		

Your Physical Equivalent

What will your physical equivalent project look like? How will you express your commitment to neighborhood revitalization at your property?

NOTE: Upgrading your night lighting must be one of the first things you do.

Your Improvement Plan

Improvement plans typically:
- Define the problem.

- Identify the standards upon which performance will be measured for each of the duties identified.

- Establish short-range and long-range goals and timetables for accomplishing change in performance/behavior.
- Establish periodic review dates.

Your neighbors are not likely to want to take on such structure. But you, none-the-less, should have some ideas to seed a New Norms discussion. What three things, if changed for the better, would lift a big burden?

1.

2.

3.

Take on these habits to help your neighborhood reach a Burn the Boat mindset.

How will you….	I'll/We'll do it by …	Who can help
Habit 1 – Respect your hood		1. 2. 3.
Habit 2 – Show up after something bad goes down		1. 2. 3.
Habit 3 – Fight disorder		1. 2. 3.
Habit 4 – Harness the collective voice		1. 2. 3.

1. What other tactics will you use to meet the object of Burning the Boat?

2. What types of New Norms do you want to institute? What will they look like?

3. Which Teams will you join? And which officer role would be most strategic for you to hold?

4. How will you measure the effectiveness of each habit?

5. How will you rid the area of drug dealers?

6. How will you respond if the house across the street becomes the victim of a drive-by shooter or vandal?

6 - Establishing New Norms

	New Norms	
	Summary	After residents decide that things must change, leaders show them a new way forward.
	Objectives	Institutionalize healthy behaviors which break down street culture and build a sense of belongingness.
	Habits to Practice	Habit 5 - Be a landlord's landlord.
	Success Milestones	Swelling of neighborhood pride.

Take on these habits to help your area reach the *We are the Champions* stage

How will you….	I'll/We'll do it by …	Who can help
Habit 5 – Be a landlord's landlord		1. 2. 3.

Who will help you model new norms?

Will you confront those who want to revert to old ways? If so, how?

		The Lag
	Summary	The period of time between when a neighborhood becomes a nice place to live and when the broader community is willing to release outdated opinions of the area.
	Objectives	• To promote the area to outsiders so they have new information to make new decisions • Increase sense of belongingness
	Habits to Practice	Habit 6 – Support annual community-building traditions Habit 7 - Promote and circulate good news Habit 8 - Support local reputable businesses
	Success Milestones	Ribbon cutting ceremonies Ability to raise rents

1. Who are the entities that you could collaborate with to help you makeover your neighborhood's image?

2. Is National Night Out celebrated in your community? Could you assist/sponsor the event?

3. Who in the press should you contact and build a relationship with?

Take on these habits to help your neighborhood get Discovered.

How will you….	I'll/We'll do it by …	Who can help
Habit 6 – Respect your hood		1. 2. 3.
Habit 7 – Promote good news		1. 2. 3.
Habit 8 – Support local reputable businesses		1. 2. 3.

I know these questions are difficult, some you may have to think about, leave blank, and answer them as you go. However, this exercise will help you grow your awareness and help you to identify resources that will help you through the lag stage by shortening the lag time and setting your expectations in a realistic manner.

Implementing the Habits

Send questions and comments to al@LeadingLandlord.com Let's work together to create an action plan for you.

100

How will you measure the effectiveness of each habit?

What else could you do to promote belongingness? (Sell t-shirt touting neighborhood pride)

How will you persuade outsiders that your area is worthy of a second look? That you're up and coming?

What TV reporters or newspaper journalist should you introduce yourself to in order to start relationship building?

How can you get the word out about what's cool in your area?

What outside groups could you start partnering with and inviting in?

Who could help you promote good news during the Lag process?

Send questions and comments to al@LeadingLandlord.com Let's work together to create an action plan for you!

NOTES

Leading Landlord Presents The Companion Audio CD:

- *6 Things You Must Know BEFORE Buying Inner City Rental Property*

- *4 Types of Inner City Landlords*

- *How to Build Equity by Investing in Your Neighborhood*

- *5 Steps for Landlords to Create a Drug-Free Neighborhood*

www.ingramcontent.com/pod-product-compliance
Lightning Source LLC
Chambersburg PA
CBHW080306180526
45167CB00006B/2691